CW01637570

AUTHOR BLUEPRINT

WRITING, PUBLISHING, BOOK MARKETING, AND MAKING A LIVING WITH YOUR WRITING

Joanna Penn

Author Blueprint

Paperback ISBN: 978-1-915425-56-0
Ebook ISBN: 978-1-915425-59-1
Large Print ISBN: 978-1-915425-57-7
Audiobook ISBN: 978-1-915425-58-4

www.TheCreativePenn.com
Enquiries: Joanna@TheCreativePenn.com

Published by Curl Up Press

Cover image created by Joanna Penn on DALL-E through ChatGPT Pro.
Final cover design and interior formatting by JD Smith Design.

CURL UP
PRESS

www.CurlUpPress.com

Contents

Introduction

There are many different ways of writing books, and many disparate paths you can take through the ever-expanding options for publishing, marketing, and making a living with your writing.

The world is changing faster than ever before, and there are lots of people sharing their experiences.

The publishing industry is no different, and in this Blueprint, I'll share my approach in the hope it will help you on your author journey, whichever route you take.

I'm Jo Penn, and I write thrillers, dark fantasy, crime, and memoir as J.F. Penn, and self-help for authors as Joanna Penn. I started writing professionally in 2008, and I left my day job to become a full-time author entrepreneur in 2011. I have over 40 books and I've sold nearly a million copies across 176 countries.

Things have changed a lot since I started out, and I've surfed the wave of disruption through the rise of ebooks and digital audio, print-on-demand, streaming and subscription models, crowdfunding and e-commerce. I intend to keep reinventing my author business as we tackle the inevitable disruption with generative AI.

I've been sharing my author journey on my blog since 2008, and on The Creative Penn Podcast since 2009, as well as in my books for authors, and in my Patreon Community.

I've learned a lot along the way! (You can find my author timeline at www.TheCreativePenn.com/timeline)

In this Author Blueprint, I want to empower you as an author and help you navigate your choices around writing, publishing, and marketing, as well as creative business.

I want you to know what's possible for authors these days, so you can make the decisions that are right for you.

I've tried to be succinct and draw together disparate sources of information from various areas so you can read it through from start to finish, or just dip in and out of the chapters if there's something you're particularly interested in.

I've also linked to my books and resources, as well as other information, so you can delve into more detail.

To be clear, I'm not (yet) a famous, multimillionaire writer! I'm just an author trying to continue writing and publishing, reaching readers, and sharing what I learn along the way in a time of great change.

I'm always experimenting, and there is an amazing network of authors online who share what they do and their results. Together, we will work our way through this new publishing world, so let's get started!

* * *

You can buy my books for authors directly from me at:

www.CreativePennBooks.com

and my fiction and memoir at:

www.JFPennBooks.com.

You can also find all my books and stories at all the usual retailers in all the usual formats.

* * *

There are some affiliate links within this book to services and products I use myself and recommend. If you buy through my link, I receive a percentage of the sale at no extra cost to you and in some cases, you may receive a discount.

I only recommend people and organizations I trust and/or products and books I've used personally, so I hope you will find them useful if you want to investigate further.

What is your definition of success?

Before we get into the main topics, it's important to take a step back, as your answers to the questions in this chapter will frame the decisions you make later. Consider these questions.

Why are you writing?

Why do you want your book published and out in the world for others to read?

Try to explore beyond your initial answers to the deeper reasons beneath and take some time to really understand why you want to pursue this.

* * *

Writers strive for different things, for different reasons, at different times — and identifying your definition of success will help you make choices about what you write, how you publish and market, and what you're willing to do for your author career.

Back in 2006, when I was miserable in my consulting day job implementing accounts payable systems, my definition of success was to leave my job and (somehow) make a living as an author.

It took five years of writing in the early mornings, building my website and podcast, and learning a lot of different skills to make it out of the job. I kept building step by step, year by year, and eventually we downsized so I could leave in 2011.

But that was just the start!

My next definition of success was getting back up to the income I had earned in consulting. That took a couple more years, but by 2015, I was earning more than the old day job, and then I far surpassed it.

My definition of success now is to keep making a living as an author entrepreneur, with multiple streams of income, so I can continue to live a creative life, write the books I want to write, and travel for book research.

What about you?

- What is your definition of success — for the particular book you're writing now, and for your longer-term writing career?
- How will you track and measure that success?
- What are the bigger reasons behind your writing?
- What will keep you going when things are difficult?

Your answers will change over time, as your definition of success will also change based on the progression of your writing career.

Here are some of the more common definitions and potential options for measuring them that may help you shape yours.

All of them are valid — and possible. The important thing is to decide what you're aiming for and then make decisions that will help you get there.

(1) It's my life goal to write a book — I want to create something I'm proud of and hold my book in my hand

This is where we all start — with the desire to finish a project and create something tangible in the world.

The book of our hearts. The story we're driven to tell. The message we just have to deliver.

The focus of success here is on the completion of a project, which is a totally brilliant reason to write a book! Creativity is its own reward.

(2) I want to get an agent and a publishing deal and see my books in a (physical) bookstore

If you want to get a publishing deal, you need to research what agents and publishers are looking for, which changes over time as trends shift. You will need to learn about the business of traditional publishing and book marketing, as well as the writing craft.

Make sure that the goals of an agent or publisher match what you want to achieve, as publishing the book is usually just the first step in a longer career.

(3) I want to reach readers with my words and change the world one reader at a time

It's great to focus on serving readers, but this definition of success is too intangible. If you only want to 'reach readers,' then you could put your book out for free on every platform in the world.

But that's not usually what people mean!

Be more specific with this type of definition. How could you measure it?

For example, is it achieved when you have fifty five-star reviews on Amazon, or you receive a fan email from a reader you've never met?

Or, if you realize you want to measure success by book sales and/or income, keep reading for examples of specific goals.

(4) I want to sell 10,000 (or whatever number) books in the next three years

This definition of success is measurable, and you will know when you get there.

But the number of books sold depends on many things. To begin with, it will depend on the genre you write, as a children's picture book will usually sell far fewer copies than a commercial romance novel, and a narrative non-fiction memoir will generally sell less than a commercial thriller.

It's also dependent on how many books you have, as you will more easily reach higher sales figures with more books, especially if they are in a series.

It will also depend on the level of marketing you or your publisher do for your work.

So choose your number carefully, based on realistic targets suited to your work, and then consider how you will get there.

(5) I want to receive critical acclaim and win a literary prize

Certain types of books win certain types of prizes, so if you have this definition of success, research the areas you want to excel in and work out what those authors did to position themselves for success.

Excellence in craft is only one aspect, as certain publishers might be the right route, and building your network is also important.

The type of book that appeals to literary critics and award judges is not usually the same type of book that has mass appeal to readers, so this definition may be incompatible with making a full-time living as an author.

(6) I want to make a full-time living with my writing

The definition of 'full-time living' differs by country, even by region. The income needs for a family with kids are different from those of a professional couple or a solo writer.

Be specific about the figure you're aiming for. Perhaps initially that will be your current salary; then consider how that may grow over time based on how much you're writing, publishing, and marketing.

This was always my definition of success, so I made the choice to self-publish and build a creative business from the beginning. I could see that it would be the fastest and most sustainable way to make a full-time living for the long-term rather than the traditional route, especially since I had already been running my own businesses in other areas. (I ran my own freelance IT consulting business for many years, as well as a small scuba diving charter, and a property investment company.)

I go into a lot more detail in my book, *How to Make a Living with your Writing.*

The full-time writing life is certainly not for everyone, as you need more skills than just the craft. But if you love learning, and you're ready to experiment, then it might just be for you.

(7) I want to create a body of work over my lifetime that I'm proud of

I am an author. I measure my life by what I create.

This is my job, but I also write for the love of creating, and I want to be proud of every book I publish — now, and until my metaphorical pen runs dry.

I intend to write for the rest of my life, hopefully for at least another forty years. I'm in this for the long haul.

The creative journey *is* the point, and there is no end game. As Stephen King says in *On Writing*:

> Writing isn't about making money, getting famous, getting dates, getting laid, or making friends. In the end, it's about enriching the lives of those who will read your work, and enriching your own life, as well.

Part 1: Writing and Editing

1.1 It's time to get started

You've spent long enough preparing, learning, thinking — maybe even procrastinating! At some point, if you want to have a finished book, you have to start writing.

Perhaps you already have pages of story fragments, or draft chapters on various topics.

Perhaps you have nothing but a vague idea.

It doesn't matter. At some point, you must start writing your first draft and wrangle that chaos of thoughts and words into something that someone else can read.

You must take this step, or you will never finish your book.

You don't need to know everything before you start. Just get going and figure the rest out later.

Your first draft won't be perfect, and you certainly don't need to show it to anyone, but at least you will have something to work with.

Things will change in the editing process, but there's a tremendous feeling of satisfaction when the first draft is done.

That feeling is your goal, so let's get into it.

* * *

This section is an overview of writing and editing. You can find more detail in my books *How to Write a Novel*, *How to Write Non-Fiction*, and *Writing the Shadow*, available in all formats at www.CreativePennBooks.com, or from the usual retailers, bookstores, and libraries.

1.2 What are you writing?

There are two ways to decide what you're writing.

The first is to start writing and see what it turns into.

Discovery writers, those who prefer not to plot or plan, favor this bottom-up approach.

The second is to figure out your genre, word count, and target audience, then write a book to match.

Plotters and outliners favor this top-down approach.

Most writers will be somewhere in between.

* * *

When I started writing my first novel back in 2009, I knew I wanted to create a fast-paced thriller with religious conspiracy elements in the style of Dan Brown's *The Da Vinci Code*.

That's the kind of book I read on the commuter train to the day job I hated. I couldn't wait to escape every day into an adventure, and that's the experience I wanted to provide for my reader. That first book (eventually) became *Stone of Fire*, the first in my ARKANE thriller series.

For some of my other books and stories, I only figured out what they were much later in the process, so don't worry if you're not sure yet what you want to write, or what genre your book or story might be.

Here are some elements to consider.

Genre or category

Genre is about understanding where your book fits into the publishing ecosystem. It's also about reader expectation, and these days, genre is just another word for 'category.'

Many first-time writers think their book is for everybody.

But it's not.

Readers like different books, and that's a good thing. It means that it's likely you will find a market for whatever you write, however distinctive, especially in a digital age when we can reach readers all around the world.

If you're worried that writing in a genre will make your book generic, don't be.

How many times have you read about two people who fall in love?

How many times have you read about mothers and sons, or fathers and daughters?

How many times have you read about characters who overcome evil and save the world?

Your story will be original because of the personal details you include, the characters you create, and the unique voice you bring to whatever genre you write in.

Some authors declare they do not want to be constrained by genre and refuse to be boxed in by conventions or reader expectations.

That's fine. Write whatever you want to.

But if you intend to publish your book, either through the

traditional or independent author route, you will have to categorize it at some point.

If you want a traditional publishing deal, you'll need to list 'comps,' or comparison titles, in your pitch. If you self-publish, you need to choose categories in order to list your book on the retailers.

If you think about this earlier, it will help you figure out where your book fits — and every book fits somewhere.

Knowing your genre can also help you with the writing process.

If you write in a genre you love and have been reading for years, you already understand the reader's expectations. You know what a satisfying read feels like, and you want to elicit that feeling in your readers.

If you have no clue about category or genre, find five to ten books that are like the book you're writing. Make sure they are modern, rather than literary classics, as the categories need to be relevant to the contemporary market.

If you can't come up with any books, then you need to spend some more time reading!

Look up the books on Amazon, scroll down to the product details section, and check the categories under "Best Sellers Rank."

Here are some examples of my books, which are correct at the time of writing. Categories can change over time, and you can be listed under more than one area.

Stone of Fire by J.F. Penn is listed under Action Thriller Fiction, Women's Adventure Fiction, and Travel Adventure Fiction.

Pilgrimage by J.F. Penn is listed under Solo Travel, Religious Travel, and Routes & Ways Travel.

Writing the Shadow by Joanna Penn is listed under Writing Skills Reference, Creativity Self-Help, and Emotions & Mental Health.

If you read cross-genre, you're likely to write cross-genre, and readers love these books, too. You don't need to be boxed in.

My Brooke and Daniel thrillers span crime, psychological thriller, and supernatural thriller categories. They don't appeal to fans of straight police procedurals, which rarely have supernatural elements, but those who enjoy cross-genre novels in this vein rate them highly.

If you follow this process for books that are like what you're writing, you'll get a clearer idea of your possible genre/s.

You can do this by manual searching,
or you can also use Publisher Rocket to
research genre categories in more depth:

www.TheCreativePenn.com/rocket

It's a useful tool to speed up the process
and you can find my tutorial at:

www.TheCreativePenn.com/rocket-tutorial

Length

The length of your book will be shaped by genre and reader expectations, or by the requirement of a competition or publisher guidelines.

Go back to your list of similar books.

Check the page count and assume around 250 words per page. Multiply together to get a rough estimate of the number of words in the book.

IT by Stephen King is a doorstopper with 1,088 pages in the paperback edition — over 270,000 words for what is a sprawling, coming-of-age, epic horror novel.

Mrs Dalloway by Virginia Woolf is a slim 108 pages, around 27,000 words, making it a literary novella.

Atomic Habits by James Clear is 250 pages, around 63,000 words, although many non-fiction books have more 'white space' than fiction, so can be shorter.

Here are some other guidelines, although, of course, there are always exceptions to the rule.

Flash fiction is under 1,000 words.

Short stories range from 2,000 to 5,000 words. If you're submitting to an anthology, a specific publication, or a competition, they will specify word count.

Novellas range from 20,000 to 40,000 words.

Novels are anything over 50,000 words, and length will vary by genre and reader expectations. Romance is often closer to 50,000 words, with thrillers, crime, and mystery usually around 70,000 to 90,000 words. Epic fantasy can stretch to 120,000 words or more.

Most popular non-fiction books are usually 50,000 to 80,000 words, but you can also find a lot of shorter books that are around 30,000 to 45,000 words.

Stand-alone, series, or serial

One book might seem a challenge at the moment, but most authors write many more over their careers. The most prolific authors in the world — and those that earn the most — often work on multiple series or write in more than one genre during the course of their careers, sometimes even at the same time. You might only have one idea right now, but don't worry, more will come.

What are the kinds of projects you might consider?

A **stand-alone** is a book that can be read on its own and is self-contained as a topic. The reader needs nothing else to be satisfied. They close the book or finish the story, and they're done.

Most non-fiction books fit under this category, although some authors also create non-fiction series grouped by a particular market with similar cover branding.

My Books for Authors can be read as stand-alones in any order, but are also grouped in series on the retail stores.

Some fictional genres suit stand-alones — for example, literary novels and horror — whereas mainstream fiction genres like romance, thriller, sci-fi, and fantasy often focus on series.

Books in a **series** are linked by a common theme, the same characters, the same world, or other elements, as well as the branding of the cover design, title, and more. Readers can immerse themselves in the books; many will binge a whole series quickly and then wait for the next one.

A **serial** is a story told in small, episodic chunks, sometimes over years, with a focus on cliffhangers and open loops to keep readers engaged.

While this is nothing new — Charles Dickens published most of his novels as serials, selling individual parts directly to readers or serializing them in newspapers or magazines — there are now lots of apps for mobile reading that make it easier for readers to subscribe.

Don't worry if you don't know what your book is up front. For discovery writers in particular, each book can have a will of its own!

When I wrote my dark fantasy *Map of Shadows*, I thought it was a stand-alone story, but after I finished the book, there was more to tell. While I had resolved the initial story arc, I couldn't leave my characters where they were.

Then I thought it was an episodic series, with the main characters having fresh adventures through different maps in each book, so I wrote book two, *Map of Plagues*, with that in mind.

But once I was midway through book three, *Map of the Impossible*, a bittersweet ending emerged and it became a trilogy. I can write more in that world, but there was a clear end to the main character story arc.

In non-fiction, *Pilgrimage* started out as a travel guide to a specific route, then morphed into a solo travel self-help book, and eventually ended up as a travel memoir and practical guide for secular pilgrims.

Yes, it would have been much more organized and simpler to have designed these books from the first page, but for me, that's the joy of discovery writing!

Which is the best option?

Only you can decide for your book, but consider what you like to read as a good starting point.

I don't read serial fiction, so I don't write it, regardless of its growing popularity, but I love reading and writing long-running episodic thriller series. As a reader, I also enjoy stand-alone novels and short stories in the horror and speculative fiction genres, as well as business books, self-help, and travel memoir, so those forms shape aspects of what I write.

1.3 How to write the first draft

When you haven't written a book before, you assume it's easy enough. This is why authors commonly hear things at parties like, 'Oh, yes, I'll write a book someday when I have the time.'

As if time is all you need!

Even after writing more than forty books over fifteen years, I still find first drafts challenging, but I've discovered some specific processes and tools to make the drafting easier — and they might also help you.

(1) Schedule time blocks for writing — and only work on your manuscript in that time

Scheduling your writing time is the secret to completing a book.

If you get your butt in the chair, or stand and dictate, for consistent periods of time, you *will* finish a draft.

Whether you want to spend that time in research, outlining or plotting, discovery writing, or editing, it doesn't matter — as long as you are making progress.

Get out your calendar and schedule time for writing, as you would for any other important commitment.

If you can't block out hours of free time, then schedule smaller chunks — even twenty minutes a day will make a difference.

Turn up for that meeting with yourself as you would turn up for a meeting with someone you respect.

Spend that time working on your book and don't do anything else during that time block.

No email, no social media, no messaging.

It doesn't matter if the words aren't great. You can clean them up in the editing process, but you need to get black on white and finish that first draft in order to edit it into something useful later.

I've used this method for years, with the free Google Calendar as my tool. I time-block everything — creative time, business admin and marketing, podcast interviews and meetings, research trips and speaking, and yes, even my personal life and fitness. It doesn't matter what tool you use, but you need to use something.

Do it now.

Get out your calendar and schedule time to work on your book.

(2) Find a location that will help you create

Our brains get used to specific locations for specific things. If you always watch TV from the couch, you'll sit down on it and automatically turn on the TV. If you use your desk at home for email or accounts, or if it's cluttered with children's artwork or unfinished DIY or craft projects, you'll find it hard to write your book there.

Sometimes, you just need to get out of the house in order to create. It doesn't matter where: a local café, a library, dictating while walking, or sitting in your car. Disrupting your existing patterns and committing to a different location can make all the difference in getting words on the page.

(3) Use timed writing sessions, or writing sprints

Once you have scheduled your writing, use the time effectively. You might be heads down for the full stretch or schedule in short breaks for coffee, stretching, or comfort stops.

Setting a timer can help you focus more intensely on the writing period. Some authors do these writing sprints with others online or in person, which helps with accountability.

You'll achieve more with multiple timed mini-sessions than if you try to write non-stop for an hour or two with no scheduled breaks, especially if you haven't yet gained the stamina for long writing sessions.

When the timer starts, don't wait for inspiration.

The Muse doesn't arrive when you sit around wishing she would. She turns up when you start creating — so get writing.

(4) Write in any order

Don't try to write the first sentence of the first chapter first, unless you have such a detailed outline it's ready to go.

You can jump around and write in any order — especially if you're a discovery writer, like me. I never write in order for fiction or non-fiction. I write scenes and chapters and thoughts and then re-order them later. Just get it all down in the first draft phase.

I use Scrivener for organizing my research, planning, and writing:

TheCreativePenn.com/scrivenersoftware

You can drag and drop the chapters around, which helps me organize the chaos of my drafts into a coherent structure later in the process.

You can watch my Scrivener tutorial here:

www.TheCreativePenn.com/scrivenertutorial

(5) Focus on writing a messy first draft

One of the life-changing moments in my writing life was when I learned that the first draft is just that — the *first* draft.

A reader will never see it.

An editor should never see it.

The first draft is for you, so make as much mess as you like.

Once it's finished and you have a coherent end-to-end manuscript, you can start editing and make the manuscript better on the next pass.

The myth of writing is that an author sits down and creates a perfect, fully formed sentence on the page, followed by another and another, until they have finished a book in one attempt.

But that's not how writing works.

You will never see the first draft of your favorite book and, as a new writer, you can only compare someone else's finished work to your first draft writing. That's not a fair comparison, so try not to do it!

Give yourself permission to write whatever you want in that first draft, knowing that only you will see it.

(6) Avoid distraction — focus on one project at a time

Writing is simple, but it's not easy.

There will always be distractions, and finishing a project has a lot to do with your ability to focus and avoid shiny object syndrome.

"Ooh look, a new story idea! That is so cool, much more interesting than this old idea I'm working on over here. Why don't I just spend a bit of time on that new, shiny story and leave the old one in the corner? I'll go back to it later."

Another common distraction is constantly learning more. "I don't know exactly how to write this character, so I'll do another course on writing characters, and then maybe one on structure just to help even further."

Of course, you need to learn, but don't spend years learning before writing. Instead, learn as you go. The best way to learn is to get professional feedback on your manuscript, but you can't do that until you have one.

Another common distraction is focusing on publishing and marketing options before you have even finished a first draft. Don't do that! There will be plenty of time to figure out the business later.

If you feel pulled to any of these distractions and give into the urge every time, you will never finish your book.

You will always have other ideas as you write. Note them down somewhere and get back to your current work in progress.

Beware of trying to write multiple books at the same time, as you may not finish any of them. Some advanced writers manage this, but if you're just starting out, focus on one.

(7) Track your progress

Writing a book can be daunting, especially if the words are hard to produce and you manage little in some sessions.

But when you break it down, writing a book is just a series of words arranged in sentences, organized into chapters, and collected into book form.

If you can write a sentence, a paragraph, or a page, you have taken another step on the journey.

Tracking your progress can help you feel you're achieving something, however small. Some authors use spreadsheets to track time writing and/or number of words. Or you can just write them on a wall chart, or note them in an app.

I keep a day book by my desk where I write a few lines on what happened each day. When I'm writing a first draft, I add a colored sticker for each writing session. My inner creative child loves stickers!

Scrivener has a Project Targets section where you can set and track word count per session, which turns green if you achieve your goal.

I also use colored flags, turning the chapters yellow when I have finished the first draft. I turn them blue after editing, and green when they are finished and ready to publish.

This makes the manuscript more visually manageable, and if I can turn one flag yellow by the end of a writing session, I feel like I have won the day.

(8) How much do you want this?

If you're struggling to find time to write, then revisit the reason you're writing. Does this book *really* mean that much to you?

We make time for the things we value.

If you're not making time for writing, then it's not high enough on your list, and that's okay, because life is difficult enough without writing a book! The only person who can decide whether it's worth the time is you.

My turning point came when I fully committed to the writing path. I stuck at my consulting job for many years, thinking that it was just what I had to do to get by. It was only when I started crying at work most days, wondering what the hell I was doing with my life, that my motivation became significant enough to make a change.

I got up at 5:00 a.m. to write, and when I returned home after work, I studied the writing craft, book marketing, and creative business, while building my author platform.

At the weekends, I cut down hobbies and social arrangements in order to have a whole day to work on my writing, and eventually moved to four days a week at my consulting job, so I had more time.

Setting aside time takes discipline until we develop a creative habit, and even then, there are tough days. Here's an excerpt from my journal in 2014:

> Today has been a difficult day. I procrastinated when I should have been writing. I emailed instead of creating things. I did busywork and admin that didn't achieve much. I spent time on social media instead of writing.
>
> I bet Stephen King wouldn't behave like this. He would sit at his desk and write something new. Today I am a tired, disillusioned misery. But tomorrow I will be an author again. I promise.

The challenge to find time is a struggle, no matter where you are in your career, but ultimately, writers write.

If you don't make time to work on your book, you are the only one who suffers, as I did in the journal excerpt above.

* * *

You can find more ideas for managing your time in *Productivity for Authors: Find Time to Write, Organize Your Author Life, and Decide What Really Matters*, which you can find on CreativePennBooks.com or on the usual stores.

1.4 Overview of the editing process

A finished first draft is just the start. Once you have the raw material, you can move into the editing process.

There are several editing stages and as you progress in your craft, you won't need every stage every time. Assess for each book what kind of editing you need along the way.

Self-editing

The self-editing stage is your chance to improve your manuscript before anyone else sees it. For some authors, this stage might mean rewriting the entire draft. For others, it involves restructuring, adding or deleting scenes and chapters, doing line edits, and more.

Developmental edit / structural edit / manuscript critique

An editor reads your manuscript and gives feedback on specific aspects of it, mostly focused on the content. An editor might address structure and flow, character and plot, and anything else pertinent to improving your book, regardless of genre.

You will receive a report, usually ten to fifteen pages, which you can use in another round of self-editing. Some editors also include comments directly on the manuscript.

While this type of editing is not always necessary, it can be a valuable step if you're unsure about the structure of your book. I had a developmental edit on my first novel when I had so much to learn, and later, I had one for the first book in a new series when I was unsure about the direction of the story. Both helped me move to the next stage.

Copyediting and line editing

This is the classic 'red pen' edit where you get comments and changes all over your manuscript.

This edit focuses on anything that enhances the manuscript in terms of writing quality and flow, word choice, phrasing, grammar, any areas that are unclear, or ideas that are not fully expressed, and more.

Some editors split this edit into two, and there are differences between what this edit is called between countries. For some editors, a copyedit includes attention only to grammar and correctness, while a line edit focuses on improving and elevating sentences.

Be clear about your expectations and make sure they match those of your editor before editing begins.

You will usually receive an MS Word document with Track Changes, as well as a style guide or style sheet and other notes, which you can then use to make revisions during another self-edit.

This is the most expensive type of edit, as editors often charge per 1,000 words based on the type of edit you want.

Make sure you have self-edited as much as you can. If you need to cut your book down by 20,000 words, do it *before* you send your manuscript for a line edit!

Beta readers, specialist readers, and/or sensitivity readers

Some authors use different readers as part of their editing process.

Beta readers can be part of the author's community and are fans of the genre. They read to help the author pick up any issues prepublication.

Specialist readers are those with knowledge about a topic included in the story. For example, a vulcanologist read specific chapters of *Risen Gods* to check the details about volcanic eruptions.

Sensitivity readers check for stereotypes, biases, problematic language, and other diversity issues and can be especially helpful if you are writing about characters with a lived experience very different from your own.

You will usually receive comments by email referring to page numbers or chapter numbers, or sometimes an MS Word document with Track Changes, which you then use to make revisions.

Many readers do this for the love of helping their favorite author with a book and a mention in the acknowledgments, but there are also paid services for specialist and sensitivity readers.

Proofreading

Proofreading is the last check of the manuscript prepublication for any typos or issues that might have been introduced in the editorial process. For print books, this can include a review of the print proof with formatting.

You should only fix the last tiny changes at this point. Don't make any major changes this close to publication or you may introduce entirely new errors.

Do you need an editor if you intend to get an agent and a traditional publisher?

You will go through an editorial process with your agent and publisher, but if you want the best chance of getting to that stage in the first place, it might be worth working with an editor *before* you submit your manuscript to an agent.

Look for an editor who will help you with your query letter and synopsis as part of their edit.

1.5 Self-editing

I'm a discovery writer, so I figure out what the book really is during self-editing. I love this part of the process, and in my self-edit, I wrangle the chaos of the first draft into something worth reading.

Shift your mindset from writer to editor, from author to reader

In the idea, planning, discovery, and first-draft writing phase, it's all about you, the writer.

You turn the ideas in your head into words that you understand, a flow through a topic that makes sense to you, and characters that come alive in your mind. In that first rush of creativity, you can banish critical voice and ignore any nagging doubts.

But now you need to switch heads.

That's how I prefer to think about it, but you might consider it as changing hats or changing jobs. Anything to help you move from the 'creative, anything goes, first-draft writer' to the more critical editor.

There is one overriding consideration in this shift. As thriller author Jeffery Deaver says, "The reader is god."

With the editing process, you turn your manuscript from something you understand into something a reader will find entertaining, educational, or inspirational.

Writing is like telepathy. It connects minds across time and space. You are reading these words and the meaning flows from my brain into your brain — but only if I craft my writing well enough. The same is true of your book.

Consider the following questions:

- Will your book have the desired effect on the reader?
- What might help improve their experience?
- How can you make sure that they're not bored or confused or jolted out of the book?
- What will make them read on and, at the end, close the book with a sigh of satisfaction and order your next one?

My self-editing process

At the end of the first draft, I print out my manuscript with two pages to each A4 page, so it looks more like a book. I put it in a folder and leave it to rest. You need fresh eyes for your edit and this 'resting' gives you some emotional distance.

I love this first self-edit, and as I'm still crafting the book as a discovery writer, I usually rest the manuscript for a week or two.

I schedule blocks of time for editing in my Google calendar and (when not in pandemic times) I go to a café when it opens first thing in the morning. I put on my Bose noise-cancelling headphones and edit by hand with a black ballpoint pen from page one to the end.

I usually manage twenty to thirty pages per editing session of a couple of hours each, but it will depend on the amount of restructuring I need to do.

I scribble notes in the margins, draw arrows to move paragraphs around, write extra material on the back of pages, or mark places where I need to write more later. I change words, rewrite and delete lines, and pick up any issues around lack of sensory detail, character problems, and more.

You can see a page of my hand-edits here:

www.TheCreativePenn.com/handedits

Some pages end up a mass of black; others are relatively clean. But in this first hand edit, no page goes untouched as I hone my manuscript into something closer to my creative goal.

You can edit on a computer or a tablet, or whatever else works for you, but at least change the font or the spacing — something to make it a different experience to reading the first draft.

Most writers have a tendency to either overwrite or underwrite, and so will either need to cut words or add words at this stage. I usually have to add chapters or scenes or deepen characters or theme at this point.

Once I've hand-edited the complete manuscript end-to-end, I update my Scrivener project with the changes. I alter the color of the flags along the way and, as ever, I back up the session and email myself the work in progress.

When I've made all the changes over multiple editing sessions, I print the complete manuscript again, and read end-to-end and edit as before.

This time, it's usually a lot cleaner and there may only be a few things to fix in each chapter.

Once I'm finished, I'll update the Scrivener project once more and then decide whether it needs a third pass. Mostly, two full end-to-end hand edits are enough for me these days, but sometimes I'll do a third or go through specific chapters one more time.

I find this messy editing process fun, and it's hugely satisfying to see my book emerge.

Don't get too hung up on the 'best' way to self-edit. You will figure out your process if you finish a draft, then jump in and have a go.

Use editing software

Once I've finished my hand edits and updated the Scrivener project, I use ProWritingAid to check the manuscript. It integrates with Scrivener, so I open my project and go through each chapter.

ProWritingAid picks up passive voice, repetitive words, commas, and typos; suggests rephrasing; and even flags culturally problematic language.

Yes, these are the type of things that an editor will pick up, but I want to hand over a manuscript that is as clean as possible so my (human) editor can focus on other issues.

I don't make all the suggested changes from the software, but it certainly helps improve my writing, and I learn as I go through. You can even create your own style guide so you spell things the same way throughout.

You can find ProWritingAid at:

www.TheCreativePenn.com/prowritingaid

and my tutorial on how to use it on your book at:

www.TheCreativePenn.com/prowritingaidtutorial

When is your self-edit finished?

You will be utterly sick of your manuscript by the end of the self-editing phase!

You have read your words so many times you can't see them clearly anymore. You are so over the whole thing that you want to forget the book altogether.

If you don't feel this way, you probably haven't self-edited enough!

When you feel you just can't do any more, it's time to work with a professional editor.

Remember, nothing is ever perfect.

You can edit forever if you keep obsessing over changes and going over and over the same material. If your self-edit goes on too long, consider whether perfectionism is holding you back. Set a completion date and hold yourself accountable to stop and move on to the next phase.

1.6 How to find and work with a professional editor

If you want your book to be the best it can be, then working with a professional editor is the next step.

An editor's job is to help you improve your manuscript through structural changes and story or topic development, suggestions for new material, line edits or sentence refinement, and so much more.

Different editors can help you in different ways, from constructing the overarching story to eliminating the final typo.

In my experience, good professional editors are well worth the investment as they help improve your book and your craft, especially in the initial stages of your writing journey. They have read so many early stage manuscripts they understand the most common problems and know how to help you fix them.

Some experienced authors only use proofreaders for their books, but personally, I still work with a professional editor on every book. I learn something every time. I am a superfan of editors!

How to find a professional editor

Consolidation in the traditional publishing industry over the last decade has resulted in many more professional editors working as freelancers, so authors have a wealth of professionals available for hire in every genre.

Check out my list of editors at:

www.TheCreativePenn.com/editors

You can also find lists of approved editors through author organizations. The Alliance of Independent Authors has a list of Partner Members, many of whom are editors.

You can also use author marketplace Reedsy:
www.TheCreativePenn.com/reedsy

Many editors use content marketing to find clients — for example, publishing articles or writing books on editing, or appearing on podcasts. Most authors also credit their editors and proofreaders in the acknowledgments of their books, and share recommendations on social media in various author communities, so it's easy to find options.

How to assess whether an editor is right for you

I frequently get emails from writers asking me to recommend an editor for their book.

But finding an editor is like dating.

You have to do it for yourself, and it's likely that you will try a few different people before you find your perfect match. You may also change editors over your writing life as your craft develops and your needs shift, and that's completely normal too.

Make sure the editor has experience in and enjoys your genre. You don't want a literary fiction editor working on your YA paranormal romance or your business self-help book.

Ensure that the editor has testimonials from happy clients, and check directly with a named author if you have doubts.

Some editors offer a sample edit for one chapter. This helps both parties decide whether the editor will be a good fit for your book. The editor can assess what level your manuscript is at, and you can decide whether their editorial style is right for you.

An editor's job is to help you make the most of your book, so if they try to steer you away from your creative vision entirely, they are not likely to be a good match for you.

How to work with an editor

When you engage an editor, you will receive a contract with a timeline and a price for the work.

You agree to deliver the manuscript on a particular date and will usually pay a deposit, especially if this is the first time you're working together. The editor agrees to deliver the edits back on a certain date and also to keep your manuscript in confidence.

You can avoid issues later by communicating expectations up front, so if you have questions about the editing process, ask before you sign a contract. Make sure your editor knows your goals for the book, so they can tailor their work accordingly. Are you writing a commercial novel that should meet readers' expectations for your genre? Or are you writing experimental fiction or an unusually structured self-help book targeted to a niche audience?

Many editors are booked months in advance, so once you know your schedule, contact them early and book a slot.

Update them if your timings change. Most allow minor slippage, but since editors plan their work around contractual dates, it's important to be timely with delivery.

Submit your manuscript and, once the edit is complete within the agreed timeframe, you will receive whatever has been agreed. That might be a structural report, line edit, or proofread manuscript, along with a style sheet.

Some editors may offer a call to discuss, but I have never spoken to an editor as part of my process as it's never been necessary. It's all about the words on the page.

If you specifically want a call, then include that in the contract up front along with anything else you're concerned about.

I consider my editor to be an important part of my team. This is a two-way relationship, and you need to behave as professionally as the editor should.

If you find an editor you love working with, pay them quickly and respect their time, and hopefully, you will have a long-term business relationship that benefits you both.

How does it feel to go through an edit?

It's probably going to hurt, especially in the beginning, when your craft is in its early stages.

But you need fresh eyes on your work, and you need feedback to improve.

When I received my structural edit for my first novel, I didn't open the email for ten days. I was so scared of what it would say because my novel meant so much to me, and yet I knew it had problems.

Of course it did, it was my first novel!

I let the email sit in my inbox until I was ready to face it, and like many things, the fear was worse than the actual event.

Even many years and many books later, I still don't open emails from my editor until I am mentally ready to face criticism.

Because that's what it feels like.

It is not the editor's job to pat you on the back and say, 'Well done, this is perfect.'

Their job is to help you make it the best book it can be. They are experts and have honed their advice over many manuscripts, so they can spot an issue a mile off.

When you receive that email from your editor — particularly if it's your first book — make sure you are well rested and in a positive frame of mind before you look at it. Set aside a good amount of time and read through the comments and the manuscript as a whole, rather than focusing on all the details. You can come back to them later.

If you have an emotional reaction, *do not* email back immediately!

Sit with the feedback for a few days, and you will find it easier to see what might need to change from a more detached viewpoint.

Once you're ready, go through the manuscript and work through each change. Don't just click Accept All on the Track Changes version for a line edit.

This takes time, but it's well worth it because you will learn with every step and you'll be able to spot your common issues in the future, and hopefully fix them next time.

Examine every suggestion to see if you want to make the change, because you don't need to accept everything. You are the author, so your creative vision is the most important thing.

But try to get some distance and assess whether the change truly serves the book, or if you're just having an emotional response.

Consider each editorial suggestion on its own merit. Does it help take the book in the direction you want it to go? Will it improve the reader's experience?

What if my editor wants me to change everything?

Perhaps they are not the right editor for you. Perhaps they misunderstood your goals for your book.

The editor should not fundamentally change your book or alter your creative vision. Their job is to help you shape your manuscript into a better version of itself, and retain your voice and ideas while improving the book for the reader. This is a skillful balancing act, which is why experienced editors are so highly sought after.

How long will the editing process take?

This will depend on the type of writer you are in terms of the first draft. If you outline in great detail and spend time up front making the first draft the best it can be, then editing might take less time than for a discovery writer who only figures out the book after the first draft.

The more books you write, the more you understand how to shape a manuscript, the more you can write a clean draft, so editing speeds up. That doesn't mean it gets easier to write a book, but it does mean you know how to find and fix issues more quickly.

It will also depend on the length of the book. A 50,000-word non-fiction book or romance with one protagonist will be a faster edit than a 150,000-word sprawling epic fantasy with multiple point-of-view characters, or a long history textbook.

It will also depend on your experience. Don't compare your editing time on a first novel to someone who has written a lot of books.

Give editing the time it needs.

You want your book to be the best it can be. But also remember Parkinson's law: "Work expands to fill the time available for its completion." This law also applies to editing.

Set your deadline and schedule your editing time accordingly. Don't book a professional editor until you've been through at least your self-editing process, as it may take longer than you think.

How much does an editor cost?

This will depend on the type of edit, your genre and word count, how experienced you are as a writer, and how much experience the editor has.

Editors usually quote a range on their website and you can also email and ask for a more detailed quote based on your manuscript's length and a sample.

Every dollar I've spent on editing has been worth it as an investment in my writing craft and the quality of my finished books. Although my requirements are different now, I continue to use editors and proofreaders. The more eyes on your book before publication, the better it will be on launch.

What if you have a tight budget?

When I started out as a writer, I had a day job and I saved up for the editorial process. It was an investment in my craft and a future creative career.

If you already have or intend to set up a business as a writer, then you can offset the cost of editing against any profits. But when you're starting out, you can't necessarily see that far ahead.

If you're on a tight budget, then find or set up a writer's group with others in your genre and work through one another's manuscripts as you all improve together.

What if my editor steals my ideas or my manuscript?

This is a common concern of new writers who think that editors might run away with their book and make millions from their idea.

But don't worry, editors are professionals. They work within a contractual framework that protects both parties. Make sure you are happy with the contract before you sign it.

If you are really worried, register your copyright before you send the manuscript to anyone else. While it is not legally necessary to register copyright — it exists the moment you get the words onto the page — there are registration companies in every country that can provide peace of mind. Just search for 'copyright registration' within your territory.

Will I need different editors when I'm further along in my writing journey?

Yes, as your craft and experience develop, you will probably work with different editors. You might also choose to use a different editor for a new genre, or work with recommended professionals to take your craft to the next level.

* * *

Resources:

- My list of recommended editors — TheCreativePenn.com/editors
- Alliance of Independent Authors Partner Member list — selfpublishingadvice.org/alli-self-publishing-services-directory
- The following editing associations offer directories and job posting services: The Editorial Freelancers Association (US), the Chartered Institute for Editing and Proofreading (UK), the Institute for Professional Editors (Australia and New Zealand), and Editors Canada.
- Interview with my editor Kristen Tate on the different kinds of editors — TheCreativePenn.com/kindsofediting

1.7 When is the manuscript finished?

You can edit a book forever if you want to.

Every time you read it, you will find things to change. Every time you hire another editor, they will find more. If you work with beta readers, they will also offer opinions.

Your book will never be finished — until you decide it is.

Nothing is ever perfect.

Even if you hire three separate editors and use multiple proofreaders, you will still find a typo or an error in the published book. Pick up any bestseller from a traditional publisher, and you will find an issue somewhere. It happens to everyone.

You must make sure your book is the best it can be, but set boundaries so you eventually finish. These questions should help:

- Have you self-edited your manuscript?
- Have you worked with a professional editor, or at least worked through the manuscript with other writers to improve it?
- Have you used editing tools and/or a proofreader?
- Have you set a deadline to move into the publishing process so you are not editing forever?

If you have been through a rigorous editorial process and you still feel the itch to edit again, be honest with yourself.

Is another round of changes really going to make a substantial difference to this book?

Would it be better to work on the next book instead of constantly reworking this one?

Are you struggling with a fear of judgment, fear of failure, procrastination, or other mindset issues that you need to work on instead of editing?

Check out my book *The Successful Author Mindset* if you think this might be the case.

Strive for excellence, do your best, and then release your book out into the world.

Part 2: Publishing

2.1 Your publishing options

There are many ways to get your book into the world and into the hands of readers. The key question is which method works for you and your book at this time, as well as what might fit into your broader long-term author career — if it's your goal to continue publishing books. It all relates to your definition of success as we covered earlier, so keep that in mind as you read on.

If you haven't finished the first draft of your book yet, don't get side-tracked by questions about publishing. The industry changes all the time, so focus on your book first, and come back to what happens next later.

If you're ready to publish, here's an overview of the main options.

(A) Personal self-publishing

Many people want to write a book for personal reasons and print copies to give to friends and family, or maybe sell at local events, or in a local bookstore.

I helped my nine-year-old niece self-publish a few years back, and we published copies for the family and also the school.

My dad wrote a mystery novel, *Nada*, which we published in ebook and print, but he didn't want to spend his precious time in retirement marketing it or running an author business.

These books are still available to buy online, but the achievement of a personal goal was more important than any other outcome.

(B) Traditional publishing

This is the established route of querying agents and submitting to publishers.

The benefits of traditional publishing include the prestige, kudos, and validation you get from making it through the process, as well as an established, professional team to manage editorial, publication, and (hopefully) the book marketing processes.

An agent and traditional publisher will not ask for money to publish with them. They will pay you royalties, perhaps even an advance against those royalties based on contractual terms, although amounts and contracts vary.

Some publishers will distribute your book to physical bookstores, and you may have a greater chance of acceptance into literary awards, as well as subsidiary rights licensing, like film and TV.

The downsides of traditional publishing include how slow the process is. Authors who go this route usually pitch multiple agents over time and often receive multiple rejections. If you do find an agent, it can take more time to get a publishing deal, and then more time before the book is out.

Royalty rates are lower because the agent, publisher, and distributors do the work of publishing and take their percentage, and there is sometimes a lack of transparency around earnings.

Some authors are disappointed by the lack of marketing for their books, and publishers inevitably move on to the next project in their pipeline. They are businesses and they need to make money, after all.

There are different traditional publishers, from imprints of huge multinational houses, to digital-first publishers, to small, independent presses specialising in specific genres. There are also varying kinds of contracts with advances and royalty rates differing between them, and agents with varying levels of experience.

If you want to go this route, do your research.

There are many different agents, and many different publishers. Learn how the industry works and how publishing contract clauses impact your career, pitch the right project to the right people, and you are far more likely to be successful.

If you are asked for money to publish, the company fits into the partnership model as below.

> For more details on traditional publishing, check out Jane Friedman's site and her downloadable chart with the spectrum of publishing possibilities:
>
> JaneFriedman.com/key-book-publishing-path

(C) Partnership publishing

In this model, the author pays upfront for services and the publisher handles all design and production tasks, as well as potentially offering marketing services.

The benefit is that you have a team to work with who know what they're doing, but the downsides include the difficulty of finding a good company to work with, as well as a potentially expensive process.

There are some fantastic companies who operate under this model, and it's especially common with non-fiction for speakers and professionals who want to turn their knowledge into words, as well as fiction authors who have more financial resources than time.

You can find vetted and recommended services in the Alliance of Independent Authors Self-publishing Services list, which ranks publishers and adds a warning if they are not acceptable. It's compiled for authors, by authors, so please check that first at:

selfpublishingadvice.org/best-self-publishing-services

White Fox is an example of a quality partnership publisher who I am happy to recommend and am an affiliate for. Find them at TheCreativePenn.com/whitefox

But as much as there are some great companies who do the best they can for authors, there are also sharks in the water — companies who operate with shady terms and conditions and rip off authors along the way. Do your research and due diligence and check all contracts carefully.

You can also check Writer Beware for publishing scams, of which there are many — writerbeware.blog

(D) Professional self-publishing — or being an indie author

In this model, the author treats the production of their book as a business, investing in professional services upfront, like editing and book cover design, as well as in marketing elements like a website, email list, and other forms of book promotion.

Distributing the book is mostly free, and the services take a varying percentage of the sale.

There are also different business models within the broader scope of being an indie author which can be mixed and matched per book, series, and/or format.

Here are the main approaches:

- **Exclusive to Amazon** through KDP Select, Audible, and KDP Print
- **Wide and retailer-centric**, using Apple, Kobo, Google, Draft2Digital, Findaway Voices, IngramSpark, and other retailers and distributors to reach readers in all online stores globally in all formats, as well as libraries and bookstores
- **Crowdfunding** through Kickstarter or other sites
- **Subscription** models like Patreon, Ream, or Substack
- **Selling direct** through an online store from simple services that deal with taxes like Payhip and Gumroad, through to full e-commerce stores with Shopify and WooCommerce. Social commerce is also emerging through TikTok Shop and other platforms.

These often represent a progression of the indie author business with authors starting out with a simple ebook on Amazon, and progressing over time to more sophisticated ways of selling books and reaching readers.

While I am not exclusive to Amazon, I use all the other methods as part of my indie author business.

* * *

The benefits of being an indie author include creative control over what you write and how often, as well as how you publish and market.

You can publish quickly and receive income much faster — within hours or days if you sell direct, or within a couple of months with the retailers.

You own and control your intellectual property rights, so you don't have to ask permission to sell your books in whatever formats you like, wherever you want in the world, using new opportunities as they arise.

You can also selectively license your rights — for example, license your books in all formats to a traditional publisher in North America and self-publish everywhere else in the world. Or license paperback only, while keeping ebook and audiobook rights.

The royalties are higher as you do the work upfront and, apart from a small cut to the distributors, you don't have to keep paying a significant amount to an agent and publisher.

You can set your own prices and profit margin, plus you can bundle deals and add different, higher-value products as you expand your business.

It's also tremendously empowering because you are in control and you can take advantages of new opportunities as they emerge.

Of course, there is a lot to learn, but if you are curious and enjoy experimenting and trying new things, you can learn how to run a successful author business. It just takes time and practice.

I have a degree in theology and used to implement accounts payable systems in a corporate job. I do not have a degree in writing, publishing, marketing, or business. I've learned everything on the job through books, podcasts, courses, consistent practice, hiring skilled freelancers, attending conferences, and by building my author network.

The downsides of going indie include the lack of prestige, kudos, and validation by the publishing industry, even if some indie authors sell more books than traditionally published peers.

Indie authors can be excluded from literary awards and competitions, as well as from certain conferences and physical bookstores.

You need to upskill, as well as find and manage freelancers to help. You also need a budget for editing, cover design, and marketing, and you need to learn how to promote your book/s in an increasingly crowded market.

If you publish direct with your own store or crowdfunding, you will need to manage taxes, customer data, and customer service as any e-commerce business must do. But you also have the benefits of a closer relationship with your readers, faster payment, and even more control.

Professional self-publishing is not for everyone, but I love (almost) all aspects of being an indie author. It suits my personality and the way I like to work. But don't worry, there are gradations of going indie. You can start simple and expand your author business as you learn and grow.

* * *

The best place to start if you want to follow this route is SelfPublishingAdvice.org, a free site written by indie authors, for indie authors.

It's run by the Alliance of Independent Authors (ALLi), which you can join to learn more and access help through the community forums. You can find guidebooks, a weekly podcast and blog, as well as a free online conference and other resources.

As Orna A. Ross, founder of ALLi, says in *Creative Self-Publishing: ALLi's Guide to Independent Publishing for Authors and Poets*:

> Being an indie author is a wonderful job, with a high level of creative and commercial freedom, but that's not to say that self-publishing is easy. To be an author, to be a publisher, to run a creative business: these are three challenging ambitions, all rolled into one indie author. You.

Which publishing choice is right for you?

You can write a book for love, but publishing is about reaching readers and in order to be a sustainable business, it has to make money.

Your creative work is valuable. Publishers are not charities, and neither are the online book platforms. They are businesses who make money from your books.

Empower yourself. Learn about intellectual property (IP) and copyright, as well as rights licensing, before you jump into a decision.

If you're offered a contract for "all rights, in all languages, in all formats existing now and to be invented, in all territories, for the life of copyright" (fifty to seventy years after the death of the author) for a few thousand dollars, you need to understand what you're signing away.

Instead, **consider selective licensing**.

This might be across different books — for example, pitching a traditional publisher with one series while self-publishing another.

While you need to pick a direction for your book at some point, you don't have to make one choice for your entire career. Many authors choose a hybrid approach, especially as they become more successful, and this can take different forms.

It might be across different formats — for example, licensing print editions while retaining ebook and audio rights. Fantasy author Brandon Sanderson kept his special edition rights while licensing the main formats to a traditional publisher, and these became the basis of his multimillion dollar anniversary edition Kickstarter.

It can also be across different territories — for example, licensing North American rights to a traditional publisher and self-publishing into the rest of the world. Or even by territory and language, like a Spanish-language edition for Spain, but not North and South America.

It can also span different time frames — for example, licensing a book for a seven-year deal and getting the rights back later in order to self-publish.

There are so many options once you understand how intellectual property and rights licensing works, which makes being an author a much more lucrative and exciting prospect!

But how do you know which way to go with your book?

Consider these questions to help you decide on your path forward.

- Do you want to write only one book, or do you want a long-term career as an author? If you want a long-term career, are you willing and able to write many more books as well as market them along the way?

- Do you want the validation and kudos that come with traditional publishing? Are you willing to play the game of submission to agents and publishers to get it?

- Do you want to make a full-time living with your books and run a business as an author? Are you willing to do the work involved, or do you want someone else (an agent and a publisher) to do everything for you?

- How much control do you want over your books and your intellectual property assets? How much do you want your independence?
- Do you love to learn new skills? Are you willing to experiment and try new things? Do you like to run projects?
- How much responsibility do you want over fulfilment and customer experience?
- Are you interested in all aspects of the author business? How much of your income will you give up in order to have other people do the work for you?

As you consider these questions, refer back to your definition of success and consider how each route might help you get there.

2.2 How I professionally self-publish

If you're just starting out, my set-up might seem complicated. But I started small back in 2008 and have expanded since then, taking each new step as I learned more and as further opportunities and platforms emerged.

You can learn any practical skill one step at a time

If you want to start simple, focus on publishing an ebook and a paperback using Amazon KDP or use a helpful distributor with good customer service like Draft2Digital and progress from there, depending on your goals as an author.

My overarching publishing strategy

I own my company, The Creative Penn Limited, which has a publishing imprint, Curl Up Press. I am the only employee, and I only publish my books (and a few for my mum under Penny Appleton).

I am open to rights licensing deals with traditional publishers, and I have selectively licensed some rights for a few books in French, Italian, German, and Korean, as well as doing some audiobook deals.

I use a **windowing strategy** for my books, releasing them in stages, which helps me make a bigger income at the beginning of a launch, as well as delivering extra value and beautiful products for my existing audience before publishing everywhere else.

For book projects, I launch on Kickstarter first with premium hardback editions, other exclusive products, and early access to the primary editions.

After that is fulfilled, at least a month or two later, I sell direct from my Shopify stores — CreativePennBooks.com and JFPennBooks.com.

If you'd like to know more about selling direct, including my lessons learned, check out my interviews and resources at: TheCreativePenn.com/selldirectresources

Finally, after another month or two, I publish wide on all platforms in all the basic formats, as well as distributing to libraries.

Here are the specific details for wide publishing per format.

Ebook

After I receive my final manuscript back from my editor, I format the ebook with Vellum, which is Mac only: TheCreativePenn.com/vellum

You can watch my Vellum tutorial here: TheCreativePenn.com/format-ebook-print-with-vellum

If you work on a PC, you can use Atticus, or there are other free and reasonably priced formatting options available: TheCreativePenn.com/formatting

Jane at JD Smith Design creates most of my covers, and you can find a list of book cover designers here: TheCreativePenn.com/bookcoverdesign

I use Publisher Rocket to find the right categories and keywords for Amazon: TheCreativePenn.com/rocket

I upload the finished ePub files to the following services, most of which are free to publish on, as they take a percentage of the sale.

- **Amazon KDP** — kdp.amazon.com. You can access all the Amazon stores worldwide through KDP.
- **Kobo Writing Life** — www.kobo.com/writinglife. KWL is for the Kobo readers and apps, as well as global partners (for example, FNAC in France or Walmart in the US), plus libraries through OverDrive.
- **Draft2Digital** — www.draft2digital.com. I use D2D for Nook, Apple, libraries, and various other ebook retailers. You can use D2D for almost all retailers, as well as print publishing if you prefer.
- **Google Play Books** — play.google.com/books/publish. I did use PublishDrive to get my books into Google Play originally, but now I am transitioning to going direct.
- **BookFunnel** — I upload to Bookfunnel.com for selling on my Shopify stores, JFPennBooks.com and CreativePennBooks.com. BookFunnel has an annual payment for their services, and Shopify has a monthly fee as well as a percentage per transaction depending on the plan you're on. You can also use BookFunnel for other direct sales options, like Kickstarter or WooCommerce.

Print — paperback, large print, hardback, special editions

You can format print editions yourself using Vellum or various formatting services, but I primarily work with my book designer Jane at JD Smith Design for interior book formatting.

You can also find freelancers for formatting and book layout in the Alliance of Independent Authors Partner Member list and on Reedsy.

I buy my own ISBNs (the price and company to do this varies by country). If you want more information on ISBNs, please read this guide from the Alliance of Independent Authors: TheCreativePenn.com/isbn

I send Jane the final manuscript and we go back and forth a few times to adjust, and then she delivers the print-ready PDF cover and interior files.

We usually do paperback and large print editions as standard and then special editions and hardbacks for specific projects. Each require different files.

I upload the files to the following places:

- **Amazon KDP Print** — kdp.amazon.com for all the Amazon stores worldwide. I do not select Extended Distribution. It's free to publish as they take a percentage of the sale. You can set your own price so you can choose what profit you make per sale.
- **IngramSpark** — IngramSpark.com for wide distribution to over 40,000 bookstores, libraries, and universities globally. They have free and paid options for publishing, and take a percentage of the sale.

- **Bookvault** — www.bookvault.app for books sold through my Shopify stores, JFPennBooks.com and CreativePennBooks.com, as well as my special editions for Kickstarter campaigns. They have varying paid options for publishing and distribution.

Audiobook

I work with professional (human) narrators as well as narrating my own audiobooks, and I am also experimenting with AI narration.

You can find extensive tips for audiobooks and podcasting in my book *Audio for Authors: Audiobooks, Podcasting, and Voice Technologies.*

I record and edit my audio files with Amadeus Pro, but you can use Audacity or Hindenburg Narrator.

Each chapter must be a separate file.

I master the files with Hindenburg Narrator, which produces the finished MP3 files to the correct specifications.

I upload the audio files to the following places:

- **ACX** — www.acx.com for Audible and Amazon. It's free to publish and they take a percentage per sale. You cannot set your own price.

- **Findaway Voices by Spotify** — www.findawayvoices.com for 40+ audiobook retailers. I deselect Audible and Amazon as I prefer to go direct there.

- **BookFunnel** — Bookfunnel.com for selling on my Shopify stores JFPennBooks.com and

CreativePennBooks.com. BookFunnel charges an annual payment, and Shopify charges a monthly fee plus percentage per transaction depending on the plan you're on. You can also use BookFunnel with other direct sales options, like Kickstarter or Woo-Commerce.

How long does it take to do all this?

Most of the work as an author is writing, editing, and marketing, regardless of which publishing route you decide to go.

In terms of self-publishing, it's certainly harder the first time you use any platform, but once you get the hang of it — and you're using the right tools and freelancers to help — it's really pretty simple.

Once I have the finished files per format, publishing means uploading them to the various services. It takes a few hours, sometimes up to a full day's work per book, depending on how many platforms and formats.

As an indie author, if I make a mistake, it's not an issue. I just fix the file and re-upload.

How does the money work?

In terms of expenses, you need to pay for an editor and a book cover designer if you want to make a quality product, but publishing on the various platforms is (mostly) free. Upload the files to the distribution platforms and they take a percentage of the sale.

For some services, you pay for a subscription or for upload, printing, or delivery, and depending on your situation, you may need to hire freelancers.

In terms of income, most services pay you monthly, up to sixty days after the end of the month in which the sale was reported. For example, if you sell a book on 15 March, you will get paid for that at the end of May.

If you sell direct, you receive income much faster, sometimes the same day or within forty-eight hours, depending on the payment method on Shopify, and within a few weeks on Kickstarter.

Every service has terms and conditions as well as help documentation and a customer service team, so please do your own research and make sure you are happy with the provider.

This sounds like a lot of work. Can someone else do it for me?

If you want someone else to publish and market your books, consider going the traditional publishing route or work with a (recommended) partnership publisher.

But if you're willing to spend time learning new skills, and if you're interested in writing more books and having more control over your author business, then you can certainly learn how to be a successful indie author.

A good place to start is the site SelfPublishingAdvice.org by the Alliance of Independent Authors (ALLi), which has lots of free articles and podcast episodes by authors, for authors.

If you need further support, I recommend joining the

Alliance of Independent Authors, which has a lot of help and a vibrant community of authors, many of them new to self-publishing, so you can ask your questions in a supportive setting. They also have a list of Partner Members, vetted services and freelancers that you can hire to help.

You can also hire freelancers who work specifically with authors through the Reedsy Marketplace, or start networking with other indie authors as we all share resources and are a welcoming community!

Resources:

- Self publishing advice from the Alliance of Independent Authors, by authors, for authors — SelfPublishingAdvice.org
- Alliance of Independent Authors — TheCreativePenn.com/alliance
- Vetted marketplace for freelancers who work specifically with authors — TheCreativePenn.com/reedsy
- Interviews on selling direct — TheCreativePenn.com/selldirectresources
- Book formatting options — TheCreativePenn.com/formatting
- Book cover design — TheCreativePenn.com/bookcoverdesign
- Editors — TheCreativePenn.com/editors

Part 3: Marketing

3.1 Marketing principles

If you ask most authors about book marketing, they are likely to grimace, shake their head, and sigh!

We are authors because we love to write, so it would be great if someone else handled the marketing. But if you want your books to sell — regardless of how you choose to publish — at some point you will need to get involved in book marketing.

This is just an overview, so if you want more detail, check out my book *How to Market a Book*, which will give you more ideas.

Here are some principles before we get into more specifics.

(1) Change your attitude towards marketing

Many authors feel that marketing and sales are dirty in some way and not for 'real' writers, but if you reframe marketing in a positive way, it will help you adopt a better mindset and make the practicalities easier.

At heart, marketing is **sharing what you love with people who will appreciate hearing about it.**

Marketing is not constantly posting 'buy my book' on social media or accosting readers in bookstores with copies of your novel. Your book is *not* for everyone, so stop trying to push it on those who are not interested.

Instead, try to get noticed by people who will love what you do and appreciate your book if they discover it.

If you can change your attitude, the whole marketing landscape will shift because it's now a positive and creative thing. If you enjoy aspects of marketing and make it part of your creative life, you'll find it works a lot better and is sustainable for the long term — it might even be fun!

(2) Don't try to do everything — and definitely don't try to do it all at once

There are so many ways to market your book, but if you try to do everything all at once, you will get frustrated. You might even burn out.

You also won't make any impact, because you'll be spread too thin.

It's important to balance your time between writing and marketing — but that doesn't mean you can ignore marketing completely! You just need to use the right kind of time, and I split mine in two.

Creative Time is when you have the energy to tap into your creativity and write.

Down Time is whatever you have left after family and work commitments, but when you're too mentally tired to create.

My Creative Time is always the morning.

When I had a full-time job, I would get up at 5:00 a.m. before work to write new words or edit because after work I had nothing left. I was exhausted.

But after dinner on week nights and in the afternoon on weekends, I spent some of that time learning about marketing and author business, and slowly putting it into practice.

I kept writing in the mornings, but I also started blogging in 2008, then I started my show, The Creative Penn Podcast, in 2009, as well as making YouTube videos. Next, I joined Twitter as my main social media site. I built my email list; I learned how to use paid advertising. I took it step by step, and over time, I started selling more books.

I cut my hours of TV and eventually moved to four days a week at my job to give myself more capacity to build my author business.

I left my job in 2011, and my pattern has continued. My mornings are for Creative Time, and my afternoons are for marketing and business admin. My book *Productivity for Authors* goes into more details, if you're struggling to find time to create.

(3) Own and build your author platform

Your 'author platform' is your ability to reach readers, and it will usually comprise many aspects, including the various marketing channels you use, as well as relationships with other authors.

But a huge following on Instagram or TikTok or YouTube — or whatever site — does not necessarily result in book sales, as you don't own the channel and if they change the rules, you can lose your reach overnight.

Authors have been through this multiple times — when Facebook Groups' organic reach plummeted, or when Amazon moved to exclusivity with Kindle Unlimited and pay-to-play advertising, or when Twitter became X and the game changed completely. Some authors use their publisher's website, but is that really future-proofed against changes in their business and your career?

I'm not saying you shouldn't use these platforms. You should definitely find those that work for you, but always bring readers back to your website and your email list.

It's best to own and control these assets as they form the basis of your long-term author business. If marketing platforms change and the industry shifts, or you switch publishers or agents or genres, you will always be able to reach readers through your email list and website.

This means paying for a domain name and website hosting. I also pay for my email provider (I use and recommend ConvertKit), and for my podcast hosting (I use and recommend Blubrry).

Remember, as the saying goes, "if a service is free, you are the product." You can always start out with free if you are bootstrapping, but consider owning and controlling your most important assets and data if you decide to take your author career seriously.

(4) Understand that you have three 'ages' and upskill accordingly

I'm forty-eight as I write this, but that is just my **chronological age**. There is also my **writing age**, which can differ by genre, and my **business age**.

These are important to consider because many authors think they should be good at something merely because of their chronological age or experience in other areas.

But an author who has won awards for their fiction and successfully traditionally published for twenty-five years can go indie and discover they don't understand how to run an author business. They may be a master at the craft, but their business age is zero.

Another author might have written non-fiction books and been a freelance media writer for years, but be back at zero when they try to write a novel.

Calculate your different ages and then consider what that means in terms of your expectations for your book and your author career.

My non-fiction writing age is eighteen, which is the number of years since I started writing non-fiction seriously for publication. My fiction age is fifteen.

My business age is twenty-four. I first set up my first business in 2000 and I had several businesses in different industries and countries before I started The Creative Penn Limited.

We are not born with these skills. We have to learn them.

After all, if you start a new job, do you expect to be successful and highly paid in year one? Or even year two or three?

Once you have five years of experience, you become more valuable and more highly paid, and you are given more responsibility. You've learned lots of different things and you've put them into practice. You have built a network of relationships in your chosen industry — and hopefully, you're more confident in your abilities.

(5) Think long term

If you're a new author writing your first book, I know how hard it is to look ahead to where you might be after you've written five more, or spent another decade writing, publishing, and reaching readers.

But if you love writing — and you get the bug for writing books in particular — then you will do this for a long time!

I started writing seriously almost two decades ago. During that time, I've changed and so has the publishing industry — and the technology has certainly shifted!

But I'm still here. Still writing, still publishing, and still running my author business.

Here are a few long-term things to consider if you want longevity in the market too.

Keep learning

Set aside time for developing your craft and also your business, as technology changes and there are new opportunities all the time.

Figure out what works for your personality and keep doing that

I tried for way too many years to become a plotter for my fiction, but I am a discovery writer, and I don't know what I'm writing until I get into the book. My creative process is about corralling a chaotic whirlwind of ideas, rather than designing and following a formal structure.

I've also tried and discarded many ways of marketing that didn't suit my personality, and leaned heavily into those that work for me — writing more books, podcasting and audio, as well as email marketing.

Whatever you choose, be consistent for the long term, as everything takes time to build.

Make friends and become part of a community

Even if you write alone and run a one-person author business, like I do, you need author friends and you need a community, people who understand this weird creative business. People who you can laugh and commiserate with, learn from, and help once you're more established.

You can do this through in-person networks and conferences, as well as online across different genres and publishing routes.

I'm a member of the Alliance of Independent Authors, the International Thriller Writers, and the Horror Writers Association, as well as less formal author Facebook groups and email lists. I also attend — and sometimes speak at — conferences in person to meet other authors and industry professionals.

It takes time to grow a network, but if you choose your community well, and invest time and energy to attend the same conferences year after year, you will make friends and also gain business opportunities.

Help others, be generous, and recommend other people's books and services if you find them helpful. Be a useful, honest, and authentic member of your chosen community.

Trust in your author brand is precious, so don't jeopardise it for short-term gain. People do business with people they know, like, and trust, and that can take years to develop.

3.2 Different ways to market your book

I frequently get asked, 'How do I market my book?'

There is no quick and easy answer, no magic bullet, only various options that you can use at different points along your author journey.

There is no 'right' way to market a book, and there are as many ways to reach readers as there are writers. We each use a different combination of what works for us, and most successful authors use varying types of marketing tactics, as well as changing things up over time.

You must find what works best for you — for each book and at each stage of your author journey.

So instead of giving you a list of book marketing tactics, here are some of the opposite polarities on the marketing scale that — along with your definition of success — will help shape your book promotion choices.

Think of each as a continuum: You will move up and down on these scales with every book as your career evolves. You'll use different elements for each launch, as well as for long-term sales.

Here are some things to consider.

Traditional versus indie publishing

Your marketing options vary based on how you publish and how much control you have over the book.

If you're traditionally published, you might be assigned a marketing team to help you or at least offered some aspects of book promotion as part of your contract. These might include an email blast, paid ads, deals in a store or supermarket, or help with pitching media for interviews and live events.

But unless you are a big name, it's likely that the promotions team will only be available for the launch period. If you want to keep your book selling over the longer term, you will need to do at least some of your own marketing.

You won't have control of your pricing, your cover, or the metadata around categories and keywords, and it won't be financially viable to do paid ads as you won't be able to measure sales and return-on-investment (ROI). This is why most traditionally published authors focus on marketing through PR, literary festivals, live events, relationships with book bloggers and media, as well as trying to build an email list and social media following.

Indie authors are responsible for their own marketing from day one, but also have control of pricing, the book cover, and metadata, and they can measure ROI with daily sales reporting. As a result, they have more freedom with book marketing, and the opportunity to do price promotions, bundling, sales description, category and keyword changes, as well as paid advertising with measurable results.

Short term versus long term

New authors with only one book will often focus on short-term sales because they can't yet imagine a future with more books.

Short-term sales are fantastic for that initial launch push, but they often cost money and are not sustainable. The spike often lasts only as long as you actively market the book or pay for ongoing traffic through advertising.

If you want a long-term career as an author, you also need to think about long-term marketing and focus on building a sustainable baseline income, money that comes in from your books consistently every month without you having to pay for it.

You need more books on the market, more streams of income, more readers on your email list, and other ways to attract and retain them. That takes time to build but is worth the investment if you want a long-term career.

Of course, most authors combine both kinds. When I do a Kickstarter launch, I have a couple of weeks going all out with marketing actions every day — emails, social media, paid ads, podcast episodes, content marketing, tapping into my networks, and more — but once the campaign is done, I shift to the more evergreen, long-term marketing approach.

Income versus brand building

Some marketing activities are about making direct income, whereas others are about brand building.

An article in the mainstream media or an interview on a radio show or a podcast with a large audience can be great for building awareness of your author brand, and as social proof for your website. Having a book launch party at a swanky location might make the local paper and give you great photos for social media. Starting your own podcast,

YouTube channel, or social media account and being consistent with posting niche content is a great way to build up a network and get attention over the long term.

But these kinds of marketing are more about building awareness of your author brand. They (hopefully) result in book sales eventually, but it will take time.

If you want to focus on immediate sales and income, use paid ads to direct traffic directly to a book sales page, measure ROI, test new variations, and iterate.

In terms of cash flow, if you want to receive money in your bank account more quickly, then selling direct can be worthwhile as you are paid within days, or even within hours, rather than months or years with traditional contracts.

Paid versus free

You will always pay for book marketing — but it's your choice to pay with either your money or your time.

Paid advertising can include newsletter blasts like BookBub or Bargain Booksy, as well as pay-per-click ads on Amazon or Meta, or hiring a freelancer to help get you media appearances, amongst many other options.

Do not pay for book reviews or files with email lists or for anything that might compromise your integrity. There are lots of scams out there, so check Writer Beware (writerbeware.blog) if you have concerns, or ask in one of the established author groups online.

I use Amazon Ads for some non-fiction books, and Meta Ads to my Shopify store for my fiction, as well as newsletter blast services, alongside content marketing.

Content marketing involves providing something for free that attracts your target reader, usually in return for an email address. Some of those people might buy other books and services from you.

I started my website in 2008 and my podcast in 2009 and — apart from hosting fees — they cost time, rather than money.

For my non-fiction books for authors as Joanna Penn, content marketing includes my weekly show, The Creative Penn Podcast, as well as articles on my website, videos on YouTube, and this Author Blueprint.

I also do interviews on other podcasts, and I have profiles on social media, although I am pulling away from active time investment in that area.

For my fiction and memoir as J.F. Penn, content marketing includes my perma-free first in series on all stores, *Stone of Fire*, and my free thriller on signup at: JFPenn.com/free

I also have the Books and Travel Podcast, which is more sporadic than The Creative Penn, but helps to bring people to my travel memoir, *Pilgrimage*. I'm also more active on social media with Instagram @jfpennauthor and Facebook @jfpennauthor, as well as Boards on Pinterest @jfpenn.

Other authors use social commerce engines like TikTok, creating multiple short videos to attract readers to their books. Investigate the options and find what works for your book/s and your lifestyle, as any marketing needs to be sustainable if you want to keep selling.

The book versus you as the author

Consider how you discover new books as a reader.

Perhaps you're at a bookstore or browsing online and a cover catches your eye, or you delve into the category or genre of books you prefer, or you search for a particular type of book with keywords.

Maybe you see an ad on social media and click through to read more. You don't care who the author is, you just know you want the book.

These are examples of **book-specific marketing**. You need a cover that will catch the eye of the kinds of readers you want to attract. You also need to put it in the right categories and use the right keywords, so they can find you. You can also explore paid advertising.

Now consider other ways you might discover books.

Perhaps you're listening to a podcast or a radio station and you hear an interview with an author and they sound interesting. Or the host recommends a book and you trust them, so you go check it out. Or you follow an interesting person on social media and they have a link to their book in their bio. Or you're at an event, and the speaker has a book that sounds worthwhile. Or you're on an author's email list, and they have a new release.

These are examples of **author-specific marketing**, reach that is based around you as a person, and more about relationships, networks, and trust in your author brand. Again, you will use aspects of both.

Stand-alone versus series

Most non-fiction books are stand-alone, in that you can read the book and you don't need to read anything else to complete the experience.

However, you can write books aimed at the same audience, use the same overall branded cover design, and tie them together with a series title, like my Books for Authors, which helps to market them online.

In terms of fiction, it's much easier to market a series than a stand-alone, as you can do price promotions on the first in series and hope to hook readers enough so they continue to read through.

I have a couple of stand-alone fiction books — *Risen Gods*, a YA dark fantasy set in New Zealand, co-written with J. Thorn, and *Catacomb*, a horror novella. They get great reviews, but they are hard to market.

My ARKANE action-adventure thrillers are easier to promote, as I have twelve books in the series, with more to come. I have a free first-in-series ebook, *Stone of Fire*, on all platforms, with thousands of reviews which I can promote with all kinds of marketing. It brings people into the series every day.

Exclusive versus wide publishing

If you are exclusive to Amazon with the KDP Select program, then you will have visibility for your ebooks in Kindle Unlimited (KU). KU has readers who will borrow, binge read, and return ebooks and audiobooks within that ecosystem. You are paid for pages read, and you can access

KU-specific marketing options like countdown deals and free days, as well as gain visibility in certain lists.

However, if you're exclusive to Amazon, you miss out on the audience of readers who buy and borrow elsewhere, including in libraries, nor can you sell direct or take advantage of other marketing opportunities.

I choose to publish wide, which means I sell my books in all formats in as many stores and on as many platforms as I can. I mainly focus on my own Shopify stores and Kickstarter since they bring in the greatest revenue, but I also use various retailers and other platforms as outlined in the self-publishing chapters. I use platform-specific, limited-time marketing (e.g., the Kobo Promotions tab or Draft2Digital promotions) every month to reach readers across the world, as well as offering bundle deals and discount coupons on my own Shopify stores.

Publish fast versus publish slowly

Publishing fast, sometimes called 'rapid release,' is a form of marketing for those who focus on Amazon and Kindle Unlimited, as the algorithm favours new content, which you can amplify with paid ads and promotions, as well as pre-orders to the next in series.

However, most authors choose to write and publish over a longer time frame, with a less frequent schedule, using launch promotions and longer-term marketing tactics. This is a more sustainable method and the way I publish.

Write to market versus write first, market later

'Writing to market' bakes the marketing into the book by writing something that will sell because there is already a hungry audience waiting to devour it. This suits authors who can write fast and adapt quickly to new niches, as well as authors who read and enjoy a specific genre and thus know it well.

Writing to market usually focuses on Amazon and Kindle Unlimited, and can work for some authors until the subcategory becomes saturated. At that point, the market becomes harder to sell in, and some writers move on to other genres.

The other approach is to write what you want to write and figure out the marketing later.

Most authors start out writing the book of their heart, the book their Muse wants them to write, the book that has been itching for years to be created.

They write that book with no thought of marketing and worry about reaching readers later. Many will happily continue in this vein, satisfying artistic needs before marketing considerations.

My books as J.F. Penn are all written for the Muse. Each project was born from my curiosity, and, as I am a discovery writer, I often didn't even know what the book would be until I finished.

But sometimes I have written to market. For example, I wrote my books for authors specifically to help others on the author journey for my audience at The Creative Penn.

Neither option is 'better' than the other. What's so fantastic about the creative world we live in now is that there's room for writers of all types, so find the method that works for you and your books.

Online versus offline — global versus local

Offline marketing is anything you do in person — speaking at a local event or school assembly, attending a networking event, or talking at a literary festival, book club, or library.

The benefits of this type of marketing include immediate sales and local brand building, as well as the possibility of becoming part of the community.

But offline, local marketing is not scalable. You can only reach people who are physically with you at that moment.

You could spend the same time writing an article or short story that could touch thousands online in multiple countries, or do a podcast interview that reaches a global market, or schedule short videos or images on social media within your niche.

I spend most of my marketing time and budget online, as it's scalable and an effective use of my time. I focus on a global audience, but I also do some speaking events and writers' festivals every year, so I meet people in person.

Introvert versus extrovert

Thanks to the book *Quiet* by Susan Cain, many writers now happily claim their introversion. I'm an introvert, which means I get energy from being alone, and I struggle with large groups, lots of noise, and overstimulating environments.

I'd rather think than speak, and I'd rather write than talk. I don't answer the phone unless it's a scheduled call. I'm INFJ on the Myers-Briggs scale, which is a rare type in the general population but far more common in the author community.

Introverts struggle with in-person marketing, book store and live events, as well as sustained periods without alone time, like the classic book tour. But being an introvert can be a superpower for online marketing. We can write and create content alone, attracting an audience online and connecting with readers through social media.

Extroverts get their energy from people, so live events in person and online are fun and energising and may be a better way for these authors to market and connect.

Digital versus physical

We can publish our books in different formats — ebook and digital audio, and then various kinds of print like paperback, hardback, large print, or special editions.

With digital products, you have more options for price promotions — for example, a limited time free or discounted deal — because there is no ongoing cost of production.

Stone of Fire is a perma-free ebook on all the ebook stores, Kobo Promotions allow discount deals, and I use Chirp Books for occasional discounted audiobook promotions. I also have digital bundles of ebooks and audiobooks at my stores, CreativePennBooks.com and JFPennBooks.com, as well as offering discount coupons to my email subscribers and advance review team.

There are fewer options for price promotions with print products as there is a cost to produce every book, so you have to market in different ways and attract readers with things that digital products cannot do. Social media favors beautiful print books as they look more attractive in TikTok videos (just search BookTok), or in Instagram images or Facebook ads.

For my Kickstarter campaigns, I produce special hardback editions with color photos, silk finish cover, metallic foil, and ribbons, and I am investigating sprayed edges and other print-specific options in future.

I have spiral-bound workbooks and print bundles for non-fiction on CreativePennBooks.com, and I offer bundle deals on both my stores for print. You can also offer signed editions, special merchandise, and more.

Data-focused versus intuitive marketing

There are two kinds of people: Those who enjoy spreadsheets and data analysis and those who don't!

I am one of the latter, but there are plenty of authors who love using data to drive their marketing, particularly in the paid advertising arena.

But don't worry, there's room for both kinds!

Data-focused marketing involves digging down into the Amazon subcategories, looking for under-served niches and focusing on algorithms, as well as analysing spreadsheets and reports for a higher click-through rate or return-on-investment (ROI).

Intuitive marketing is more about doing what feels right for you and your book, and trusting that you will attract readers over time. Of course, you have to do some kind of marketing in a sustainable way for the longer term, but this approach is more individual.

Back in 2008, when I started out trying to market my first book, I made it onto national TV and into the papers, but I didn't enjoy the spotlight, and I needed something sustainable I could do from home. I also had no author friends, so I started my show, The Creative Penn Podcast, well before podcasting went mainstream.

I enjoyed it, so I kept going, even though it took years to grow a listenership. Now my podcast is the engine of my non-fiction book business, but only because I leaned into my intuition and did something I enjoyed and could sustain for years.

I do some paid advertising, but I use Amazon auto-ads, which optimise themselves, and I outsource my Meta advertising so I don't have to manage the optimisation.

However, there is some data I focus on — my income and bank balance. I am a businesswoman as well as an intuitive creative!

I highly recommend *Dear Writer, Are You Intuitive?* by Becca Syme and Susan Bischoff if you're interested in discovering more. Becca and I also discussed intuitive writing and marketing in an interview on The Creative Penn Podcast.

Fiction versus non-fiction

While many kinds of marketing — such as email marketing, paid ads, and social media — can work for all books, there are some kinds of marketing that are more effective for fiction versus non-fiction and vice versa.

For my fiction under J.F. Penn, I mostly focus on marketing the first books in my various series, using perma-free and price promotions on ebooks and audio, as well as box sets and series bundles, and Meta paid ads.

I'm also expanding into print special editions and merchandise as part of my Kickstarter campaigns, and my store, JFPennBooks.com.

For non-fiction, I focus on marketing print and audio with higher-priced products, as non-fiction readers are less price sensitive than fiction readers, although I also have ebooks available.

In terms of content marketing, for fiction, I have a free thriller, a free first-in-series book, and plenty of books and stories so readers can find me, as well as limited social media.

For non-fiction, my content marketing is mainly my podcast and articles on the website, online interviews, professional speaking, as well as having a series of books.

Doing your own marketing versus hiring professionals

There are many people and services you can hire for book marketing, but you need to consider two questions:

First, is it worth doing?

Second, is it worth paying for?

For example, is it worth paying someone to run your Amazon Ads for you when you can set auto-ads running without intervention?

Is it worth starting a TikTok channel if you hate watching videos?

Is it worth paying a PR professional to get you interviews in magazines when you are just starting out and you're unsure of your brand?

Over the years, I've mainly done my own book marketing, learning new skills, trying things out, and pivoting along the way. But I have paid professionals at different times for different things.

At the time of writing, I pay a freelancer to format my podcast transcripts, and I have also outsourced Meta ads to my store, JFPennBooks.com.

If you want to hire a professional, be specific about what you want, as well as your timeframe. Examples of specific advertising strategies might be 'Run Meta Ads for three months to the first book in my fantasy series' or 'Pitch media outlets for three months around my non-fiction self-help book on dealing with anxiety.' You will also need a budget.

If you want help with book marketing, you can hire vetted professionals from the Reedsy Marketplace and find people in the Alliance of Independent Authors Partner Member list.

* * *

I've touched on just some of the options for book marketing, but don't worry — you don't have to learn everything all at once.

Think about what might be right for your book, for your personality and lifestyle, as well as for this particular period of time in your author career.

Book marketing is not optional — you cannot just publish a book and expect it to sell — but you have the choice of what form that marketing takes.

Pick something and give it a try, and you can learn more and pivot over time.

Resources:

- Articles and free information on marketing — TheCreativePenn.com/marketing
- *How to Market a Book* — Joanna Penn
- *How to Market a Book: Overperform in a Crowded Market* — Ricardo Fayet
- *How to Self-Publish and Market a Children's Book* — Karen P. Inglis
- Book marketing ideas from the Alliance of Independent Authors — Selfpublishingadvice.org/category/marketing-promotion/
- Hire book marketing professionals from the Reedsy Marketplace — TheCreativePenn.com/reedsy
- Alliance of Independent Authors Partner Member list — Selfpublishingadvice.org/alli-self-publishing-services-directory/

Part 4:
Making a living with your writing

4.1 Step by step into your author career

If you want to make a living with your writing, it's certainly possible. But there's a lot to consider, so these questions and principles should help you think more deeply about it.

Do you *really* want to build and run an author business?

Go back to your definition of success from the beginning of the Blueprint.

Will running an author business help you achieve that success?

While you can certainly make some money with your writing without running a business, making a 'living' requires a more focused approach.

Many authors want to make money with their books, but they are often not interested in learning the skills required to make it happen. They don't have the patience for the long-term game of writing and reaching readers over the years it takes to grow a successful business.

There are easier ways to make money than writing and selling books, but for those of us who love this business, there is no other way we want to do it! But it's worth asking the question and spending some time journaling on your answer. If you commit to this path, your reasons will help you through the difficult times.

Are you ready to learn new skills and invest in yourself and your business?

Even if you have decades of writing experience, you are back at square one with running a business. It requires a different skill set to the craft side of being an author. So much so that I split my calendar into separate writing and business time slots, and I think about it as if I am changing my hat or my role to become someone else.

Jo, the artist and author, is very different to Jo, the businesswoman, and I need both to be successful in the arenas I have chosen. Over more than fifteen years, I've spent time and money investing in both these roles, learning the skills I need to expand my capability for better craft — and better business.

To be successful, you need a "growth mindset," as Carol Dweck called it in her book *Mindset: Changing the Way You Think to FulFil Your Potential.* You must believe that you can learn and grow and change, rather than being stuck where you are right now forever. You need to see challenge as an opportunity, constructive criticism as a way to improve, and effort as more important than any innate talent. Continuous learning must become a way of life.

Yes, you need to keep making time to write and develop your craft. But if you want to make a living with your writing, you also need to develop your business skills.

Your attitude towards money is also an important aspect of the business mindset. If you don't believe you can make money with your writing, then that will be true for you.

If you think authors who make six- and seven-figure incomes are 'selling out,' then you're never going to make that amount, because it doesn't align with your values.

If you don't think you're good with money, then educate yourself.

If you have a negative attitude towards wealth, then work on changing that mindset. Start with my recommended books at TheCreativePenn.com/moneybooks

For more mindset tips, check out *The Successful Author Mindset.*

What kind of business do you want?

If you're determined to take this route, then you need to consider what kind of business you want to build.

The most successful traditionally published authors run businesses, and so do the most successful indie authors, but we all run different kinds, and you need to find what's right for you.

A traditionally published author might work with an agent to license their rights in various formats, territories, and languages, as well as subsidiary rights like film and TV. Their income will usually come through their agent, who receives it from the various publishers and licensors.

Some traditionally published authors have their own imprints within publishing houses, and they hire professionals to help with marketing. Some even start different companies to run aspects of their business.

For example, JK Rowling started Pottermore Publishing in 2012 as the global digital audiobook and ebook publisher of her Harry Potter and Wizarding World books, while she licenses the print editions to traditional publishers.

Indie authors often have multiple streams of income from different retailers for different formats, all arriving at different times. I'm paid every day for my Shopify sales, every month for most of my retailer sales, every quarter for my licensed books, and every campaign for my Kickstarters.

Many authors, both traditionally published and indie, also have other forms of income that develop from their book businesses, including professional speaking and teaching in person or online, freelance writing, ghost writing, editing or other related services, consulting or coaching, physical products and merchandise, affiliate income from recommending books and services, subscriptions or tipping from fans, and advertising revenue or corporate sponsorships.

These multiple streams of income are important to protect your business over the long term. The world changes, the industry changes, companies change, and so do you. Don't put all your eggs into one basket, as the old saying goes. I know this from hard-won experience.

Back in 2008, I was an IT consultant at a mining company, and on one particular day, hundreds of us were laid off as part of the disruption of the global financial crisis. Our senior manager came in with a stack of letters and we were called in one by one to get them before leaving the building.

On that day, I realised I was dependent on one company and they had just taken away my only stream of income. I had no control over the decision and I was unprepared for the sudden change in circumstances.

I swore then I would never let that happen again, and over the years since, I've grown multiple streams of income as part of my creative business.

My book income is spread across multiple genres, series, and formats, as well as multiple retailers and distributors in multiple countries who pay me directly. A growing proportion is from direct sales on my Shopify stores and Kickstarter campaigns.

I also have podcast sponsorship from companies, Patreon subscriptions, and affiliate income. I can turn other streams — such as consulting sessions, professional speaking, live in-person events or online webinars — on and off as I need them.

Any business goes through ups and downs, and it's important to hedge against the down times. I also invest outside of the publishing and tech industries, so I have some protection from sector-wide fluctuations.

What is a 'living'? How much money do you want to make?

When people think about making a living with their writing, they often assume they will write one incredible book, get a traditional publishing deal with a huge advance, then a movie deal, and all the trappings of success. That is the dream and, in many cases, the myth of publishing. We hear stories of outliers getting seven-figure debut book deals and, of course, there are tales of amazing success, but that's not the reality for most writers.

The top 1 percent of authors, the ones you know by name — like Stephen King, James Patterson, JK Rowling — are certainly making a lot of money, but most authors are not earning anywhere near that amount.

In 2023, the Authors Guild in the US reported that for "full-time authors whose books are in commercial markets (i.e., excluding academic, scholarly, and educational books), the median book income was $15,000 and median author-related income was $25,000."

In 2022, the UK Authors' Earnings and Contracts survey reported that primary occupation authors (those who allocate at least 50 percent of their time to writing) had a median income of £7,000 (around US$8,500).

In April 2023, the Alliance of Independent Authors Income Survey reported that the median income of "primary income" self-publishing authors (those who spend more than half their working time on writing and publishing activities) was $12,749. This figure comprised authors who were making over $80,000 and those who brought in under $1,000 in a year.

None of those median income figures are what I call a living, and some people might find those surveys disheartening.

But I understood the reality when I decided to become a full-time author entrepreneur back in 2006, and there was only one way to think about it.

Don't be average.

Be the outlier.

If you want to exceed the amount of money that so many authors earn, you have to do two things:

First, decide how much you want to make.

Second, decide what you will do to reach that.

What are you going to do to achieve your goal that sets you

apart from the average author? How can you do that every year so your business is sustainable?

Find someone to model

When I decided to leave my job and become an author entrepreneur back in 2006, I knew it was possible because I could see others who were living the way I wanted to.

Those role models made it possible to believe that I could do it too, and I still have people I follow for that reason.

Find people who make an income doing what you want to do. Read their books and articles. Listen to their podcasts. Join their email list and/or community. Go to their events and buy their courses. You might even be able to pay for consulting. You could also email them, but respect their time and only ask intelligent questions after you've been through all of their publicly available material.

You also don't need to find just one person to model. Consider finding different role models across various aspects of your potential future business. My sources for learning about the craft of writing are different from those I use to learn about podcasting, email marketing, Shopify sales, or Kickstarter.

Curate the voices you listen to with care and consider whether the advice is relevant for the direction you want to go.

Some careers cannot be modelled because times have changed. A traditionally published author who started out in the 1970s or the 1990s will have a different view of the publishing industry than an indie author who started in the 2020s.

An editor in a publishing house on a fixed salary can tell you what their imprint wants to publish, but they can't tell you how to make multiple streams of income from your intellectual property assets.

If you want to write a YA romantasy series and then drive traffic to your books through TikTok, definitely don't ask me how to do it!

If you find someone you want to model, look at the full scope of their business and lifestyle and consider whether you want to embrace that direction.

For example, you might see an indie author who is always high in the Amazon charts, but you discover they spend most of their time writing to chase the algorithm and most of their revenue on paid ads, making little sustainable profit.

Or you might see a traditionally published author in the paper or in the news, maybe one who's even won a prize, but when you dig into their financials, you find they teach an MFA course as a day job, and their book makes little money.

You might find another indie author who writes one book a year, sells direct through Kickstarter and Shopify, doesn't hit any bestseller lists or make a splash on the retailers, but who makes a comfortable six-figure income selling to their readers.

Your craft and business role models will change over time as you grow in experience and confidence. Perhaps you will even be a role model for others in the future.

Start selling something as soon as possible

If you want to make a living with your writing, then you need to put your words into the world. You can take the first step with something small — like a short story or a short non-fiction ebook — but you need to take that step.

If you don't already make any income from your writing, then get started. Prepare something for sale and actually sell it.

Making that first ten dollars from someone you don't know is magical, because if you can make ten, you can make a hundred, or a thousand — then you can do that every month, or even every day.

You will learn by doing, and your confidence will grow.

Expand your multiple streams of income

If you're already making some money from your writing, then start expanding your possibilities. Where are you leaving money on the table?

For example, if you're traditionally published in the UK/Commonwealth, you could self-publish in the US and other territories.

If you have non-fiction ebooks and paperbacks, have you considered audiobooks and workbooks? Or could you turn the material into an online course? Or a live event?

If you write fiction, how could you bundle your books for better deals if you sell direct? Or do a crowdfunding campaign for a beautiful special edition? Or work with other authors to do a limited-time digital box set that will earn as well as cross-promote your books within a genre?

You can also increase your income by growing your audience.

Having more readers will lead to more book sales.

Bringing more traffic to your website will result in more sales of books and courses.

Increasing the number of engaged subscribers on your email list will lead to more sales and an ability to sell direct and make higher profits.

How could you improve your marketing to make the most of these opportunities?

Focus on one area, learn the tools and technology, then apply them to your creative business, one step at a time.

You'll find lots more ideas in my book *How to Make a Living with Your Writing: Turn Your Words into Multiple Streams of Income.*

Find your community

I still remember how lonely I was in the early years of my writing journey. I lived in Brisbane, Australia, and none of my IT consulting friends understood my desire to write. I didn't know any other authors, and when I eventually found some writing groups, people looked down on me for self-publishing.

I started podcasting to connect with people further afield, and I found virtual friends on Twitter, some of whom are now my friends in real life. It took time, but now I'm part of a thriving community that understands the challenges of writing and of running a creative business.

However resilient you are, you need a community of writers who understand the challenges you will face. As much as your family and friends love you, they are not your ideal readers, and they won't understand the inevitable creative and business hurdles we all have to tackle along the way.

You need people who will support your choices and your definition of success, as well as help you in the difficult times. As you develop, you will also be able to lend a hand to those coming after you.

There are many organizations for authors and writers, so research the ones that might work best for you. I'm a Member of ITW (International Thriller Writers) as well as the Horror Writers Association as my genre-specific groups.

I'm also an advisor and active member of the Alliance of Independent Authors, an international organization for indie-minded creatives.

Choose the groups that work for the direction you want to take, and curate the voices you listen to.

If you're in a group where people are negative and tear you down, then find somewhere else. There are plenty of wonderful, supportive groups full of empowered creatives with an abundance mindset, making money with their writing. You will find your community. It just might take a little time.

Plan the transition to writing full time — if you want to make that shift

You certainly don't need to be a full-time writer to make money from your words, and in fact, many people enjoy their jobs and write as a side hustle. This takes the pressure off making an income with your art.

But if you want to go full time, as I did back in 2011, then it can be done. Remember, however, it's more of a slow growth curve than an immediate shift. Don't quit your day job and expect an income from writing next week!

I started writing in 2006 and it took me five years to build my author business on the side before I could leave my day job. We also sold our house, downsized, and paid off all our debts. In addition, we saved six months' income in case I didn't make any money at all. It took another four years before my writing business income exceeded that from my old day job.

If you want to follow the same path, start by planning to replace 10 percent of your monthly salary with writing income.

Write down what that is for you.

Now do some basic sums. If you can make $3 profit from the sale of a book, how many books do you need to sell in a month to meet your target?

It will be difficult if you only have one book, but what if you have five books in a series in multiple formats?

What if you add in some other streams of income?

Once you're making 10 percent of the number you want to achieve, you can decide on your next step.

You can find more detail on taking your author career to the next level in *Your Author Business Plan.*

Think long term

There are easier ways to make a living than as an author, and it's certainly not a get-rich-quick scheme. The goal is to create a body of work that you're proud of and that creates an income for the long term.

It takes time to learn your craft.

It takes time to learn the principles of creative business and put them into practice.

It takes time to build an audience and find your place in the community.

But you're a writer. You love writing. What else do you want to spend your life doing?

Take it word by word, step by step, year by year.

Since I went full time, I've repeated the same pattern: I write and edit my words, I continue to learn about the craft and creative business — and, importantly, I put that knowledge into action.

I've made a lot of mistakes, but I keep moving forward. I love my creative career and if you want to take this path, it's definitely possible.

Resources:

- *How to Make a Living with Your Writing: Turn Your Words into Multiple Streams of Income* — Joanna Penn
- *Your Author Business Plan: Take Your Author Career to the Next Level* — Joanna Penn
- *Business for Authors: How to be an Author Entrepreneur* — Joanna Penn
- My Author Business Community on Patreon — www.patreon.com/thecreativepenn

4.2 Thinking ahead: The impact of AI and other technological changes

Technology marches on, and we have a choice to embrace it and use it, or stick with the old ways and potentially get left behind.

When I started my university degree in 1994, we went to a physical library to check out physical books; we hand-wrote our essays, and they only built a public computer room in my final year. There was even a vote taken as to whether we should keep the pool table instead, since no one could see much use for computers in academia.

When I started my first professional job in 1997, it was the early days of the internet. I had a pager before I had my first (dumb) mobile phone, and Amazon was a new company.

When I started writing seriously in 2006, the iPhone and the Kindle had not yet launched. You could sell PDFs online, but the concept of ebook reading and digital audio was unknown. There was no easy way to sell print-on-demand books, and audiobooks were all on tape or CD.

When I left my job to become a full-time author entrepreneur in 2011, we were still on 3G mobile. Instagram was brand new, and AI was mainly in sci-fi books and films.

As I write this in 2024, generative AI tools are going mainstream with use cases from discovering new medical technologies and materials, to modelling the climate, generating marketing copy and ads, programming, counselling, career advice — and yes, writing.

If you want to avoid AI tools completely, then go analogue. Write by hand or with an old-school typewriter and get off the internet.

But if you're considering how to use AI tools in an ethical, creative way, then read on.

What does generative AI mean for us as authors?

Whether you think AI tools can generate human-level words now, or whether you think it might take a few more years, it's clear that the models are improving every month.

Some authors are in denial, and others are suing the creators of the tools.

Some authors are angry and anxious — and many are afraid.

But some of us are embracing this new wave of technology, using it to amplify our creativity and help achieve our unique creative goals.

As an overarching principle, I'm a techno-optimist, and I only have a full-time creative career now because I've adopted the latest tools, technologies, and platforms along the way.

In my career, that has consisted of digital publishing — ebooks, audiobooks, and print on demand; internet and mobile business; email marketing and social media; crowdfunding and direct sales e-commerce, as well as using the companies and services that have sprung up within those sectors.

I'm keen to adapt and change as the opportunities shift once more, and AI tools are the next step.

Is it pointless to write if AI can do it all for us?

I've been asked this a lot lately, but the question implies that the point of writing a book is only for the output, the finished product.

You could use AI to write your book. You could use a human ghostwriter if you like.

But why would you want to?

The point of writing is a deep exploration into the themes and topics and worlds you want to investigate, as well as into yourself. It's about the process of writing, the skills you learn, and experiencing a roller-coaster journey that will turn you into a different person over the months and years you write.

Personally, I write to make sense of the world. I write to connect with others, and when I finish a project, I'm proud to hold the finished book in my hands and say 'I made this.'

I measure my life by what I create, and I want to build a body of work I'm proud of over my years of being an author.

So yes, I make a living with my writing, but I don't write books and stories just for the money. I'm experienced enough with the AI tools that I could generate a book a day if I wanted to.

But I don't want to, because that really does feel pointless.

However, I will use the various AI tools to help me expand my imaginative possibilities and achieve my creative goals.

The AI-Assisted Artisan Author (or A4)

An artisan can be defined as "a worker in a skilled trade, especially one that involves making things by hand," or one made "in a traditional or non-mechanical way using high-quality ingredients" (*Oxford English Dictionary*).

I tried to find a better word than artisan and no doubt some will argue with my use of the term, but I think it works because I intend to personally oversee and hand-craft my books and products while also incorporating AI writing and creativity tools into my process, as well as using the marketing and business services available.

I aim to produce books of even higher quality and work with the AI tools to go deeper into my themes and write in an ever more personal way. As Anaïs Nin said, "If you do not breathe through writing, if you do not cry out in writing, or sing in writing, then don't write, because our culture has no use for it."

Because it's not about the faster production of words and paragraphs.

It's not about creating ever more 'content.'

It's about meaning and the connection between you and your reader.

Of course, you don't have to use AI tools for writing, but you still might want to use AI-powered marketing and business tools. Here are just a few that authors use:

- ChatGPT for marketing copy, business planning and analysis, and book recommendations
- DALL-E or Midjourney for ad images, social media, and book trailers
- ProWritingAid or Grammarly for editing
- Amazon auto-campaigns and Meta auto-targeting for paid advertising
- AI-powered marketing algorithms on sites like TikTok, Instagram, and Facebook, as well as sales algorithms on Amazon and more.

There are more options every week, and given that Microsoft is rolling its AI Copilot into Word, and Google is expanding generative AI into Docs, pretty much all the tools that authors use will soon be integrated somehow with AI.

As more and more content is generated by AI, here are the ways you can double down on being human and connect with your readers in an ever more authentic way in order to stand out.

Write the books only you can write and include personal elements that can only come from you

The goal is to make every book resonate with your humanity even as you use AI tools as part of your creative and business processes.

If you're writing non-fiction, fill your pages with personal stories, not just tips that could come from anyone.

If you're writing fiction, explore the personal themes that keep you awake at night, or delight you and make you laugh, or help you escape into another world and inspire a sense of wonder. Center your humanity and put more of yourself into your work.

I know how hard this is. Fear of judgment is my deepest struggle — with my books, with my podcast, and especially on controversial topics like this!

I was scared to publish my crime thriller *Desecration* for fear of what people might think of my darker side. I was worried when I published *Writing the Shadow* as I shared personal stories that revealed elements of my life I'd kept hidden.

Even after fifteen years of being an author, I was terrified of publishing my *Pilgrimage* memoir as it laid bare my midlife depression and thoughts I hadn't even shared with my husband, let alone the wider world.

But we need to tap into these personal aspects.

Because AI tools can generate unlimited words in very little time, and never tire, never stop.

You can't beat the machine — but that doesn't matter.

Your books are the sum of your ideas and your writing. Your prompts. Your curation. Your editing.

Your creative direction.

However you create — with or without AI tools — it's more important than ever to find your voice and reach readers as one human connecting with another.

Create beautiful books and physical products

While digital products (ebooks, audiobooks, online courses) will continue to be important as an option for readers, generative AI will result in digital abundance, which will drive revenue down as there will be so much supply.

If you think it's hard to stand out in a crowded market on the big retailers now, just wait until the wave of generated books hits the stores.

Scarcity will become ever more precious and important, and making beautiful physical books and products that take effort and money and time to create will delight readers and fans, earn you more money, and help you stand out.

In 2023, I produced my first beautiful limited-edition hardbacks as part of two Kickstarter campaigns.

For *Pilgrimage*, I produced a hardback with my color photos from the walks with silver foil on the inner cover, a flyleaf cover with a silken finish, and premium paper.

For *Writing the Shadow*, we used gold foil on the flyleaf cover and a black ribbon, as well as a silken finish.

Both were signed and exclusive to the limited-time campaigns, although both books are available in the other formats from my stores, and also the main book retailers.

These premium physical products are an expression of my desire to make something beautiful for these books of my heart. They delight readers — and also make me a decent profit!

They satisfy my artistic and business goals and help my books stand out from predominantly digital only AI-generated books.

I intend to publish more beautiful books in the future and I have loads of ideas about future creative projects. I consider this an opportunity rather than a threat.

Foster connection and community with other humans through your marketing

Share aspects of your personal life that would be hard to replicate consistently over time with AI tools.

Yes, there are already deep fake photos and photo-quality AI images of people who don't exist — but you are real, so share real photos on social media or your website, preferably with your face and your voice so people can see and hear you.

Of course, you need to protect your boundaries.

I don't share pictures of my husband on social media, but I share enough pictures of my cats and other random things regularly that you know I am a real person with a varied life. It's not all about branding, or on-message photos like the kind generated by fake media purely for sales purposes. It's about human connection.

Be a human with a physical body

Attend events in person so you can meet and connect with other humans, which will help you build and maintain a network of people who know you are real. That sounds weird, but over time, this social graph will become ever more important.

I know this is hard. I'm an introvert with an edge of social anxiety. I'm sensitive to sound and light, and find crowds and noise difficult.

I have to schedule days of rest before and after in-person events and often leave early when it all gets too much. But this kind of person-to-person connection is critical, and increasingly so as the digital world becomes even more pervasive. People do business with people they know, like, and trust, after all.

After fifteen years of building a digital, scalable, online business, I'm now searching for connections that are more physical and immediate. Less scalable, more personal.

Of course, it can be expensive and impractical to travel to events and conferences, so try arranging a meet-up locally with other authors, or organize a reader event at a local library. Or consider how else you could do something in person. What might intersect with your books, stories, or world?

Sell direct so readers connect you, the human, with your books (and other products)

When you sell direct, you develop a closer relationship with the buyer. You can create and distribute beautiful physical books and products; you also control your profit and get paid more quickly. You can email readers over time, fostering the relationship — and yes, encouraging more sales!

You're also able to focus your marketing on sending readers to your store, where you control the customer experience and there are no other books competing for attention as there are on the big retail stores.

While my books are available in most formats in the usual places as well as available to order in bookstores and libraries, I focus mainly on selling through my Shopify stores and Kickstarter campaigns these days.

You can buy my books for authors at www.CreativePennBooks.com and my fiction and memoir as J.F. Penn at www.JFPennBooks.com.

These are just some aspects of doubling down on being human, and I'm sure more will emerge as this industry changes and shifts over time.

Are you ready to adapt?

Indie authors are successful right now, but the old model is shifting, and I know I need to change in order to be successful for the next fifteen years of my author career. I'm only forty-eight. I have a lot of life left in me (touch wood!).

At an author conference last year, someone described me as one of the 'old guard' of indie because I've been doing this for so long. I'm grateful for the opportunity to surf the wave of digital disruption over the last fifteen years — but I also don't want to be the 'old guard.' I want to be in the vanguard of this new exciting movement full of authors and creators forging their path on the back of this *next* wave of technology.

So I'm experimenting and playing and trying new things. I'm pushing the boundaries of my existing creative process and, slowly, I am shifting into being an AI-Assisted Artisan Author. How about you?

Resources:

- More interviews and information at: TheCreativePenn.com/future
- The AI-Assisted Artisan Author — TheCreativePenn.com/a4
- AI for Authors: Practical and Ethical Guidelines from the Alliance of Independent Authors — selfpublishingadvice.org/ai-for-authors-guidelines/
- Join my Patreon community for tutorials on AI tools like ChatGPT, Claude, DALL-E, Midjourney, and more — www.patreon.com/thecreativepenn

Your next steps

I hope you've found this Blueprint useful — that you're buzzing with ideas and excited about the opportunities ahead!

You may also feel a little overwhelmed, and that's totally normal.

Remember, you don't have to do everything at once. Take it step by step.

Step 1: Decide what to focus on next and then take one small step in that direction

Stop overthinking. Stop adding more to your to-do list.

Simplify.

Decide on one concrete thing that will make a difference, then do it.

If you need to finish the first draft of your book, sit down to write.

If you want to build your email list, choose an email provider and set up a simple form.

If you want to self-publish on Amazon, log into KDP and start going through the screens.

One day, or even an hour, of practical experience can propel you forward far more quickly than trying to learn without doing. Pick an area and learn as you go.

Step 2: Plan your time and keep turning up for those appointments with yourself until you achieve your focused goal

If you need to finish that first draft, reorganize your schedule.

Clear space to write, then turn up to that appointment with yourself as you would to any important meeting with someone you respect.

Once you've achieved that goal, you can move on to the next step.

Finished a first draft? Great! Start the editing process.

Set up a basic email form? Great! Start learning how to bring readers to it, so they sign up.

Implement the next step once you've finished the last one. Don't do too many different things at once or you will get overwhelmed.

You don't have to work on this every day, or even every week, but if your author career is important to you, then make time for it. Otherwise, another year will pass and you won't be any closer to your goal.

Step 3: Keep going, be consistent, and keep a long-term perspective

Patience on the journey is hard, especially as you see other authors achieving the success you seek. Creativity is its own reward and you will (hopefully) find writing a satisfying way to spend your time, regardless of the external outcome.

But you might also find that over the long term, you can achieve a great deal.

Back in 2006, before I started writing, my life was very different.

We lived in Australia and I worked as an IT consultant implementing accounts payable systems. I wrote technical specifications at work and journaled at home.

I had no books, no readers, no website, no podcast, no blog, no social media, no YouTube channel, no professional speaking business, no author friends.

I had no income from my words.

I had nothing but a day job I hated and a dream to escape and somehow make a living with my writing.

Almost two decades later, I've written and published more than forty books, and I've sold almost a million copies across 176 countries and six languages. I'm an award-nominated, *New York Times* and *USA Today* bestselling fiction author and an award-winning creative entrepreneur with a multi-six-figure business based around my writing.

None of this could have happened without small actions taken almost every day, consistently for years.

I love writing, and I love my job as an author entrepreneur.

Your journey will not be the same as mine, but if you want to join me on the path ahead, you just have to take the first — or next — step.

Happy writing, and all the best with your books!

Thanks,

Jo

Want more help?

Want more from me?

- You can buy my books in all formats from CreativePennBooks.com (non-fiction for authors) or JFPennBooks.com (fiction and memoir), or from whichever store you shop at in your preferred format.
- Tune in to my show, The Creative Penn Podcast, on your favourite podcast app every Monday. You can find the backlist and links at TheCreativePenn.com/podcast
- Join my community on Patreon.com/thecreativepenn for video tutorials, patron Q&A audios, behind-the-scenes discussions, and more. It's the price of a coffee a month (or a couple of coffees if you're feeling generous).
- If you want to connect on social media, you can find me on Facebook or Instagram @jfpennauthor, or (sometimes) on X @thecreativepenn

Need more help?

- Check out SelfPublishingAdvice.org, which has free articles, podcast episodes, and resources written by authors, for authors.
- Join the Alliance of Independent Authors (ALLi), which provides advocacy, contractual help, and a vibrant community and forum for independent authors — www.TheCreativePenn.com/alliance
- If you need to hire freelancers to help you with writing, publishing or marketing, check out the list of ALLi Partner Members — selfpublishingadvice.org/alli-self-publishing-services-directory/
- You can also find vetted freelancers on the curated Reedsy Marketplace — TheCreativePenn.com/reedsy

Books by Joanna Penn and J.F. Penn

Writing Craft and Mindset Books for Authors — by Joanna Penn

How to Write a Novel

How to Write Non-Fiction

Writing the Shadow

The Successful Author Mindset

Business Books for Authors — by Joanna Penn

How to Make a Living with your Writing

Your Author Business Plan

Productivity for Authors

Audio for Authors

Public Speaking for Authors, Creatives and Other Introverts

Business for Authors

Successful Self-Publishing

How to Market a Book

Career Change

Artificial Intelligence, Blockchain, and Virtual Worlds

The Relaxed Author —
co-written with Mark Leslie Lefebvre

The Healthy Writer — co-written with Dr. Euan Lawson

Co-writing a Book — co-written with J. Thorn

Buy direct at www.CreativePennBooks.com

Or find my books in all formats on your favorite retailer

ARKANE Action-Adventure Thrillers — by J.F. Penn

Stone of Fire #1
Crypt of Bone #2

Ark of Blood #3

One Day In Budapest #4

Day of the Vikings #5

Gates of Hell #6

One Day in New York #7

Destroyer of Worlds #8

End of Days #9

Valley of Dry Bones #10

Tree of Life #11

Tomb of Relics #12

Short story: Soldiers of God

Spear of Destiny #13

Brooke and Daniel Psychological/Crime Thrillers — by J.F. Penn

Desecration #1

Delirium #2

Deviance #3

Mapwalker Dark Fantasy Adventures — by J.F. Penn

Map of Shadows #1

Map of Plagues #2

Map of the Impossible #3

Short Stories — by J.F. Penn

A Thousand Fiendish Angels

The Dark Queen

Blood, Sweat, and Flame

A Midwinter Sacrifice

With a Demon's Eye

Beneath the Zoo

Other Fiction — by J.F. Penn

Catacomb

Risen Gods — co-written with J. Thorn

American Demon Hunters: Sacrifice — co-written with J. Thorn, Lindsay Buroker, and Zach Bohannon

Travel memoir

Pilgrimage: Lessons Learned from Solo Walking Three Ancient Ways

Buy direct at www.jfpennbooks.com

Or find my books in all formats on your favorite retailer

About Joanna Penn

Joanna Penn writes non-fiction for authors and is an award-nominated, *New York Times* and *USA Today* best-selling thriller author as J.F. Penn.

She's also an award-winning podcaster, creative entrepreneur, and international professional speaker. She lives in Bath, England with her husband and two British short-hair cats, and enjoys a nice G&T.

Joanna's award-winning site for writers, The Creative Penn, helps people to write, publish, and market their books through articles, audio, video, and online products as well as live workshops.

www.TheCreativePenn.com

Buy my books direct
www.CreativePennBooks.com
www.jfpennbooks.com

Listen to my podcasts
www.TheCreativePenn.com/podcast
www.youtube.com/thecreativepenn
www.BooksAndTravel.page/listen

Find me on social media
www.Instagram.com/jfpennauthor
www.Facebook.com/jfpennauthor
www.x.com/thecreativepenn

Printed in Great Britain
by Amazon

40271104R00079